DESTINATION
GALAPAGOS

by

Gwen Moore

TURTLE PRESS

Port Townsend, Washington

2011

Destination Galapagos
by Gwen Moore

Published by
Turtle Press
P.O. Box 158,
Port Townsend, WA 98368
(360) 385 3626

Book design by Ruth Marcus
Sequim, WA

ISBN: 978-0-9651963-0-7

This book is dedicated to Pat,
who had the dream,
and to "Heather,"
who gave it life.

AUTHOR'S NOTE

This is a true story. Five well educated, ostensibly sensible adults really did fly, in a single engine plane, from Santa Monica, California to the Galapagos Islands and back. The account is written from my point of view, but many of the recollections and some of the words belong to Pat Britt. I am deeply grateful for her generosity. I have lost track of the others over the years, but my appreciation of what they brought to the venture has increased with each safe trip I have taken. They taught me more than I knew. Their names have been altered to avoid invading their privacy.

CONTENTS

PROLOGUE

I have a faded snapshot of the five of us. The lighting is dim—it was a cold drizzly morning—but the familiar outlines of our rented Piper Cherokee-6 are clear. So are the fools who are about to fly it from Santa Monica, California, to the Galapagos Islands.

Joe, the pilot, is on the wing, waving the approved flight plan awkwardly above his head. David towers over Heather, his hands protectively on her shoulders. He looks proud, as well he might. The day before he had installed an auxiliary gas tank in the cabin to give us adequate fuel for the over-water hop. Heather, uncomfortable in the cold caress of wet khakis, smiles through clenched teeth. Pat's face is almost hidden—she is tying her shoe-laces—but her childlike frailty gives evidence to the ravages of her recent illness. I'm at the edge of the picture, looking my worst in old paint clothes, hair plastered around my head like a skullcap, tossing a champagne glass to one of our unseen friends.

The laugh on my lips is black humor. This trip had me scared to death. There was no earthly reason for us to be going in a single engine plane. Even in '73, before the heavy onslaught of tourism in the Galapagos, there were numerous scheduled flights into Guayaquil, Ecuador, that connected with the twice-weekly charter flight to the islands. Ours was an incredible act of folly.

I keep the photo in the corner of my mirror to remind me of the rewards of folly.

Our "crew" and the Cherokee-6 dwarfed by a 747 at
Panama International Airport.

"...You feel yourself then to be really on a journey
in the fullest sense of the word; not just a shifting
of the body from point to point but a journey that
moves through all conceivable dimensions of space
and time, and beyond. For a voyage to a destination,
wherever it may be, is also a voyage inside oneself."

Larens van der Post, *Venture to the Interior*

CHAPTER ONE
Los Angeles, California

1. The dream

It started with Pat's dreams of wildlife and wild places. Even as a child, she was obsessed with Africa and the "tortoise" islands. She read extensively about expeditions, field studies, and adventures, but filled her life with more practical matters: earning a Ph.D. in mathematical logic, finding a job in computer technology, buying a home. Travel was on hold until later.

"Later" took on new meaning as she struggled to regain her strength after a life-threatening recurrence of rheumatic fever. Dreams were more important than careers. They required equal time. She bought her dream car—a red MG—and started searching for an adventure.

I share a house with Pat, so she told me all about her plans. They bored me. I was depressed. Everything bored me. 1972 was my year to come unglued. I had been quite thorough about it, quitting my job, retreating to a mountain cabin, playing hippie in Mendocino, getting Rolfed at the Esalen Institute in Big Sur, having an affair with a faceless pharmacist from Glendale, and finally returning home to work with a cuddly bear of a psychologist. I was numb. Pat's enthusiasm didn't touch me.

Undaunted, she signed up for a UCLA Extension class on the Galapagos Islands. The documentary movies whetted her appetite, but the proposed tour, a few days on a large boat with sixty people, wasn't what she wanted. The trips touted in travel magazines were similar. Impatient with delay, she ignored her doctor's warnings and joined a photographic safari to East Africa.

While she was gone, I found a programming job. Progress, yes, but there was still an empty void in my life. I couldn't touch the piano, and music is my first love.

2. The adventure

Pat returned from Africa with 33 rolls of film. I was amazed at the beauty of her first attempt at wildlife photography. Eager to talk about her experience, Pat invited Heather, a chemist from UCLA, over for a slide show. I enjoyed Heather. Her cool laboratory demeanor could melt into outrageous humor in a second. Position and income to the contrary, she was still the free-spirited eighteen-year-old who had left her country home in England to wander the world. Backpacking through Europe and the U.S., she had found her way to Berkeley where she earned her Ph.D. Now she had her own research lab. But she missed the excitement of her travels and was eager to hear about Africa.

"It was everything I dreamed of and more," Pat told us.

"So the safari was perfect," Heather exclaimed.

"Not perfect, no. I saw Africa's wild beauty, but I couldn't touch it."

"Whatever that means," I said.

"Everything was under glass. Look, there were twenty-five people, including three very proper ladies in their eighties. They wanted a comfortable, pretend adventure, not the real thing."

"So what's adventure?" I asked. "For those people, that trip was it."

"I'm talking about my version of adventure," Pat replied. "No controlled outcome. I have to tempt fate."

Heather set her beer mug down with a thud. "That's a bit extreme. Adventure is freedom. Freedom from itineraries, schedules, that sort of nonsense. Adventure is relying on my wits."

"You make a great team," I said. "Why don't you plan a Galapagos trip?"

Heather laughed. "You'll live to regret that challenge."

"Probably. But while you're plotting, I'll just check the chicken—" I headed for the kitchen.

"Wait," Pat called after me. "I forgot to tell you about the Galapagos tour the Sierra Club is sponsoring. They're using three small sailboats."

"How many people?" I asked.

"Fourteen."

"Really!" Heather's two-octave, three-syllable, pronunciation said it all.

"Now there's a trip even I can handle," I replied. "Let's do it. You two can have your adventure another time. Damn! What do you suppose is burning?"

3. The boat

Pat sent off deposits for the three of us, but soon received word that the trip was fully booked. I was relieved, but Pat and Heather were devastated. Over drinks, they leafed morosely through the Sierra Club literature.

"It's such a shame," Heather mourned for the third time. "That was exactly the right trip for us."

"They must be doing it every year." I was trying not to sound pleased. "Let's sign up for the next one."

"I suppose you're right. But listen. The brochure says the smallest sailboat, the Bronzewing, sleeps six. It's owned by a man named Julian Fitter, and here's his address. Maybe he'd rent it to us."

"That's ridiculous, Heather," I said. "None of us knows how to sail."

"The boats must have crews," Pat replied. "The Sierra Club can't have been planning to staff them with tourists. That's a great idea, Heather."

"And it'll be cheaper to rent directly from the owner."

"Not if just the three of us go," Pat pointed out. "We'll have to find at least two more people."

"Actually," Heather said, "I have two friends who want to see the Galapagos."

"Anyone we know?" I asked.

Heather licked her lips. "David, for one."

"Your new lab assistant? You told me he just graduated."

"He'll be twenty-five in April."

"Won't he have fun with us forty-year-olds."

She glared at me. "Age isn't important. We share a great many interests."

"I see." I thought for a moment. "He's moved into your apartment?"

"Next week."

"And here I thought you liked older men. Who else wants to go?"

"A computer nut named Joe. He's a friend of David's, but he's our age."

"I think it's time we met David and Joe. Why don't you bring them here Sunday night? Ask them—no—tell them I'll cook chicken."

4. The people

I liked David immediately. Handsome and outgoing, he had an inquisitive mind. He questioned us closely about the behavioral characteristics of our many animals before he was even inside the door.

"For heaven's sake, come on in. Let me get you something to drink." I led him into the kitchen and handed him a beer. "So. You're working in Heather's lab."

"Best job I ever had."

"I'll bet. And are you going on to graduate school?"

"No. I've had enough of academia. I can learn what I need to know right there in Heather's lab."

"But you won't be qualified to teach," I said.

"That's a plus. What about you? Are you a musician or a programmer?"

"Both." I paused. "Neither. Sometimes."

"You're not sure? I couldn't live with that level of ambiguity," David said.

"Neither can I. Ah, here comes Joe after the guacamole. Or are you after a beer?"

"Uh, sure, I guess so." Joe smiled but didn't meet my eyes.

"He wants a beer," Pat said, "and why is everyone standing in the kitchen? Let's go sit down."

We followed her obediently into the dining room, beers in hand, and settled into an awkward silence. Finally, Pat said, "So you guys want to go in with us to rent the Bronzewing?"

"Sounds like the perfect way to learn about the islands." David helped himself to a fistful of chips.

"Well then, you're on," Pat replied.

"Actually," Heather said, "I've been thinking about it and maybe we should wait until next year."

"Why on earth?" Pat asked.

For a moment no one spoke. Then David said, "From what I've heard, the only way to see anything down there is to hike around, and, well, Heather says you can't manage that, Pat. Why not wait until next year when you'll be stronger?"

"I don't believe the doctors, but they're telling me there won't be a next year."

David thought about it for a minute. "That's a good reason. One last big fling. I'll buy that. But why the Galapagos?"

"If I go back far enough, I suppose it's because I've always wanted to ride a Galapagos Island tortoise."

"I don't think they let you," I said.

"And when I read about them, the islands sounded like a kind of reptilian Eden. Gradually I realized that they are a living textbook of evolution, and—"

"You mean the Darwin discoveries?" Heather asked. "The way the creatures on each island are specialized?"

"Yes. And there's something else, something undefinable. All the authors mention the power of the islands. They speak of enchantment."

"But from a scientific point of view," Heather said, "what's interesting is which of the creatures are endemic—"

"Excuse me, people," I said. "I want to check the chicken. Joe, can I get you another beer?"

"I'll get it." He followed me into the kitchen.

I lifted the aluminum foil and poked the chicken with a fork. "Tell me, Joe, why do you want to go on this crazy trip?"

"I've...you know, spent too much time in the computer room and it's...I'm forty and it's time to...to see more of the world."

I shoved the broiler pan back into the oven. "Heather says you're a pilot. You must have seen some of it from your plane."

"Yeah. And the more I see the more I want to see. Know what I mean?"

Joe relaxed as he talked about flying, and I relaxed, too. By the end of the evening, we were friends. At the door, he shook my hand warmly.

Heather paused on the doorstep. "We're agreed, then? I'm to write Julian Fitter about renting the Bronzewing?"

Joe smiled. "Okay by me."

The rest of us nodded.

"I'll do it," David volunteered. "I can use the typewriter in the administrator's office."

"There's no reason to ask her," I said. "I have a typewriter right here—"

"At midnight I don't have to ask."

"Oh," I replied, startled. "Well I guess we'll just leave it to you." I waved goodbye and shut the door. "Does he mean what I think he means?"

"Yes," Pat replied.

"How strange. So, Pat, your dream is in safe hands."

"Creative hands, yes. Beyond that, I'm not sure."

5. The plane

Heather and David's combined organizational abilities were considerable. They made short work of the charter arrangements, reporting in less than a month that the Bronzewing and its crew had been reserved for three weeks in December. Ten months would give us plenty of time to prepare, and I was looking forward to a leisurely sail around the islands.

But it soon became clear that chartering the boat was only the beginning. We were in the middle of our Sunday night chicken ritual, listening to an account of their recent flight to Baja California, when Heather exclaimed, "I have a splendid idea. Why doesn't Joe fly us down?"

"To Baja?"

"C'mon, Gwen," David said. "To the islands. The Galapagos."

"The Galapagos?" I gasped. "And why not? They're only— what, 650 miles off the coast of Ecuador. Joe can manage that, can't you, Joe?"

"Uh, sure," he replied. "I can, you know, practice up on Catalina."

"Really, you people are impossible," Heather exclaimed. "I'm serious. If we flew down in a small plane, we'd avoid all that red tape with the charter flight, and save money besides. Joe, tell them how it was in Baja."

He grinned. "It was great. We'd take off and just cruise around. We had the place to ourselves—"

"And no schedule," David interrupted. "When we spotted a bird or driftwood on the water, we'd go in for a look and skim along over the waves. Unbelievable." He reached for more chips.

"That's the way to travel," Pat said. "We can land anyplace that's long enough and camp or go beachcombing. Won't that be fun, Gwen?"

"Not for me, it won't. If you idiots are planning to fly to the Galapagos in a little windup toy, count me out."

"You don't trust my flying?" Joe looked hurt.

"I have no quarrel with your flying. It's the whole idea. For starters, Pat has to have oxygen if we go over five thousand feet—"

"No sweat," David said. "I can install a tank for her."

"And when she uses it up—"

"We'll refill the tank. You won't need it all the time, will you, Pat?"

"No. Just for emergencies."

"Right," I said sarcastically. "Joe, how are you going to get us into your three-seater?"

"We'll rent a bigger plane," David replied.

"You do that and I'll go."

I wasn't worried. No one would rent us an airplane for a trip to the Galapagos. But even if Joe managed to talk some fool into doing it, there was still the matter of gas for the return flight. We would hardly find aviation fuel for sale at the nearest tortoise pond. Sure that I was on safe ground, I joined them in a toast to the journey and put the whole thing out of my mind.

6. The gasoline

My friends greeted me one night with shocking news: Joe had rented a Cherokee-6.

"I find it hard to believe anyone in his right mind would rent you a plane to fly to the Galapagos Islands," I grumbled.

"Not the Galapagos," Joe laughed. "We're flying to Ecuador. The owner wasn't interested in details like where we were going inside the country."

"There's still the little problem of insurance," I said, my confidence flagging.

"We have it," David smiled smugly.

"And I suppose you've arranged to have gasoline sent out to the islands for our return flight?"

"We're writing that letter tomorrow night," David said.

"To whom?" I asked.

"The Equadorian military. Someone in that organization should be willing to do that for us."

"I'm sure they'd be delighted to help," I said, struggling to my feet.

"Is anything wrong?" Heather asked.

"I just can't believe this is happening."

"But you said you'd go," Joe whined.

"I know. I know." I escaped to the kitchen, opened another beer and tried to think. Nothing I said was going to stop them. They were determined to make this happen. And I had agreed to go.

7. The visas

I wasn't surprised when, three weeks later, David announced that the Ecuadorian Government had agreed to ship two barrels of aviation fuel to the islands.

"That's the least they could do," I said, in a desperate attempt at humor. "So are we all set now?"

"No," David replied. "The next step is to get permission to land in Colombia, Ecuador, and every country in Central America. And you're going to help me do that, Gwen."

I took a day off from work to follow David through the embassies in Beverly Hills and downtown Los Angeles. I find red tape terrifying, but David was unfazed. By the end of the day, we had completed the paper work for all the visas and filed letters about landing in each country. He was elated. I was exhausted.

"I had no idea how hard it would be just to find the embassies," I said. "Getting this trip together is a bummer."

"It's been like this every step of the way. You have to really want it."

"I know. You do. I don't."

"You said you'd go."

"I'm not complaining, just trying to get used to the idea."

"You'd better hurry. We're on our way."

8. The life raft

When our planning sessions got around to the purchase of emergency equipment for our over-water hop, I knew departure was getting close. Heather and David wanted to buy a life raft from Sears. We said great, get it and stock it.

Delighted, they approached this project with their usual thoroughness, putting together a complete survival kit: life vests, medical supplies, concentrated food, crude fishing gear, a solar still—everything we'd need if we ditched in the ocean somewhere between Guayaquil and the islands.

My colleagues at work were horrified that I was going on a trip with these crazy fools. "It's one thing for Pat," one of my friends said over dinner. "She's dying, anyway, so it doesn't matter. But why are you going?"

"I guess because I said I would. It's too late to back out."

"That's ridiculous," he replied. "You'll get killed and for what? Look, if they have to fly down, why not take a two engine plane? It would be a lot safer, and I'd feel better about it."

At our next Sunday night get-together, I brought the subject up.

"What?" said Joe. "That guy must be an idiot. Do you know what happens to a two engine plane when one of the engines kicks out? The plane goes in a circle."

"It does?" I said. "I had no idea."

Joe laughed, but I didn't get the joke. And that answer, when conveyed to my worried friends, caused even greater alarm. They were making me very nervous, but I still felt that I had given my word and must continue on.

9. The itinerary

It was in this frame of mind that, one night in October, I came upon the four of them on the floor in the study, crawling around on a set of maps. Joe had a piece of string long enough to represent convenient refueling distance for the plane. He was holding one end of it on Santa Monica and moving the other end in an arc over a second map.

"That's good," he mumbled. "We can enter Mexico at Hermosillo and go on to Los Mochis for the night."

"Is this a joke?" I yelled. "If I'm going to risk my neck, I'd like to treat the itinerary with a little more respect."

Joe ignored me. "Now from Los Mochis, we can refuel in Puerta Vallarta and spend the night in Acapulco."

"Don't you people see how ridiculous this is?" I asked.

"You said you'd go." Pat looked wounded.

"Not with a harebrained itinerary. It's bad enough to be

leaving in the middle of a gas shortage. I had to sit in a line for three hours this morning to get half a tank of regular."

"You got it, didn't you?" Heather asked. "Besides, gas isn't a problem in Mexico."

"But what about— Oh, forget it."

I listened in silence as they completed the itinerary, then turned to the next pressing issue.

"O.K., there it is," David said. "Seven days to Baltra. Now about the shots: we need yellow fever, smallpox, cholera, and tetanus. UCLA does all of them except yellow fever. For that we go to Long Beach."

"Pat, tell me again what film you're using," David said.

"Has anyone bought snorkeling gear?" Joe asked.

"How many books are you taking?" Heather wanted to know.

"No books," Joe said. "Now listen carefully. The weight limitations on this airplane are severe. I will not take off if anyone has more than twenty pounds of luggage. It's much too dangerous. Is that understood?"

10. The final details

In the rush to tidy up loose ends at work, we didn't start packing until the last minute. That was Friday, November 30, 1973, and it was a night to remember. I arrived home depressed after a cocktail party. My colleagues were sure they'd never see me again. They had promised to bronze my computer terminal as a memorial.

Our friend Alan had reluctantly agreed to house-sit. He had just returned from Nepal, and we hadn't had a chance to brief him about the house. Our plan was to do that over dinner and then look at his slides. But he had many stories to share and slides to show, and it was late before we turned to the house-sitting details. We gave him a fresh beer before telling him he would be feeding two large dogs, four cats, three turtles, multiple fish, an African rock python and several smaller snakes, the rats for the snakes, the pet tarantula and her private cricket colony. That finished, we turned to the intricacies of watering our three acre hillside lot, the problem of transporting trash to the top of the hill where he would also find the mail and paper, and a multitude of other details.

A bearded Swarthmore dropout-turned-programmer, Alan was agreeable to all of this. He responded by nodding, requesting another drink, and instructing us to write it all down. At midnight, we said goodnight and started writing.

The document required more work than we had realized and when we finished, at 2 a.m., we really didn't care whether we had any clothes on the trip or not. Sleepily we began dumping whatever came under our hands into a pile in the middle of the house.

I started jamming clothes into the nylon 'stuff bag' normally used for my sleeping bag. "If we're camping on the way down, we won't need resort wear." I picked up a pair of ancient jeans. "I'm going to take old paint clothes. After all this planning, how come I don't know what to pack?"

"You weren't paying attention."

"What's your excuse?"

"I know what to pack. I just haven't done it yet."

"I think it's an omen."

She didn't respond. I pushed the thought out of my mind.

The mess around my feet was real. I couldn't pretend any more. In a few hours we would be on our way. We had become the dream.

CHAPTER TWO
Santa Monica, California to Mexico

1. Leave taking

T he screech of the alarm was only slightly less welcome than the door chimes. Alan was hung over.

"That was a great dinner."

"I'm surprised you remember," I said.

"Why not? Tell me, did I really agree to feed Pat's snakes?"

"'Fraid so. It's not bad if you don't make friends with the rats."

"I'll remember that. So," he pointed at the bags by the door, "are we taking this trash to the top of the hill?"

"That's our luggage."

"Stuff bags and paper sacks? You're traveling incognito?"

"As bag ladies," I said. "We didn't start packing until 2 a.m."

"How come? You've been planning this trip for a year."

"No, I've been dragging my feet for a year. And then I was too scared to pack."

"I'd be scared, too," he said. "It's a suicide mission. Look, Gwen, you don't have to get on that plane."

I shook my head. "I had a year to say no and didn't do it. They're counting on me. Alan, will you take care of the animals if we—if we don't make it?"

"Write that down," he smiled crookedly.

"Hey, I'm serious."

"I know. I'll see to them." He gave me a hug and helped me into the car. "Greetings, Patricia."

"Hi, Alan." Pat climbed into the back seat. "The snakes ate. You won't have to feed them until next Saturday. And one word of advice: don't make friends with the rats."

"And here I was going to whip up some rat mousse tonight. Now I'll have to eat the whole thing myself."

"Invite the neighbors."

"You do these little get togethers regularly? So, where to? The Santa Monica Airport?"

"First we stop at the top of the hill. I'm leaving notes for the neighbors. They might like to know who's inviting them for dessert."

2. Santa Monica Airport

Joe had given me directions for finding the plane. I had them clutched in my hand, sure that at least this part of our adventure was under control. Yet, when we pulled in beneath the SANTA MONICA AIRPORT sign, we were completely lost. The instructions didn't make sense, and Joe was nowhere to be seen.

"Left or right, Gwen?"

"Either. He doesn't say."

"Let's try straight ahead. It's got to be here someplace. I'll just drive along slowly and you guys look for something familiar. He gave you the registration number, didn't he, Gwen?"

"Well, yes. It starts with an 'N'. "

"So does every other plane registered in this country," Pat said.

"It ends with 56W. We ought to be able to see that."

"All you have to do is look for a Cherokee-6," Alan said. "When you spot one, I'll stop and you can take your time checking the numbers, right?"

"Right," I said, trying not to sound as dispirited as I felt. Neither of us had as much as seen a picture of a Cherokee-6. And as for the registration numbers on the tail, even the largest of them was hard to read through the rain that was starting to fall heavily around us.

The honking of a horn behind us startled me. It was a carload of friends who had been following us. "Where the hell are you guys going?" Steve yelled.

"Not sure," Alan replied. "Follow us!"

"I think we should just go home," Pat said.

"Wait," Alan yelled. "Isn't that Joe's car just pulling in?"

"And Heather's right behind him," I said.

Joe waved happily as he passed us and led the way to the plane, unperturbed as usual by the miscommunication he had caused.

We parked close to the Cherokee-6 and jumped out into a wet drizzle. Joe was unlocking the side door of the plane.

"Hurry, Joe," I said. "The rain's starting to come down hard."

"Yeah. I'd better go check weather. I may have to file an instrument flight plan—"

"Wait just a minute here. What are we supposed to do?"

"Weigh everything. There's too much stuff here." He started off toward the terminal.

"O.K., but hurry. We can't pack without you. Hey, guys, we have to weigh our stuff—"

Pat nodded. "Good plan. Look who just pulled up. Jerry, greetings!"

Confusion mounted as more friends arrived. In their eagerness to help, they began systematically emptying our cars. I tried to stop them, but they ignored me. I was relieved when David appeared in the center of the group. He looked calm and reliable, like an old Ford truck.

"Thank God," I exclaimed. "Now we can get things under control."

"You're in the way." He dropped a duffel bag on my toe.

"Our stuff's getting wet, David."

"A little water never hurt anything."

I moved aside and watched them dump sacks, boxes, sleeping bags, water bottles, and anything else they could find into a soggy pile. I tried to rescue a paper bag filled with apples, but the bottom fell out. I noticed that my snorkeling gear stood naked, its protective sack shriveled up around its feet. The storm was ripping away a layer of reality. My own feet were freezing. I looked down and watched the glue give way on my desert boots. I was searching for my sneakers when David reappeared. He dropped a sleeping bag on the pile.

"You're going to get wet down there on the ground," he said.

"Really?"

"Yes. And you'd better start packing. That stuff's getting soaked." He started toward the terminal.

"Wait!" I scrambled to my feet. "Where's the scale? Joe wants us to weigh everything."

"Heather has it. Make sure no one has more than twenty pounds."

"David, we can't pack the plane. We don't know how. Joe says it isn't safe to take off with full tanks and an unbalanced load—"

"So make sure it's balanced. Heather knows all about it."

Pat and Heather were just coming around the back of the plane. "I know all about what?" Heather asked.

"Balancing the load."

"Actually, I don't know a thing about it."

"Where's the scale?" Pat asked.

"At home." Heather wet her lips. "I forgot to pick it up."

A door slammed. "The cars are empty," Alan announced. "Shall we start shoveling this into the plane?"

"We have to do it scientifically," I said. "You guys have been wonderful, but there's no point in everyone catching pneumonia. Why don't you take a break?"

"O.K., if you're sure. Give a yell if you need us."

I watched enviously as they headed for the hot coffee. "This is a nightmare," I said to Pat. "How are we going to load this water-logged stuff without Joe and David?"

"What's the big deal?" she replied. "Just get it inside."

"But the weight distribution—"

"What Joe doesn't know won't worry him," Heather said. "Grab those sleeping bags."

Pat and I stuffed them into a small compartment in the nose of the plane. When we returned to the side door, we found Heather inside. "Have you met our plastic friend?" She pointed to the polyethylene container. "Now we're all set for the over-water hop."

I stared in astonishment. "That's the gas tank? I expected something smaller."

"It holds thirteen gallons—"

"But it's enormous. It almost touches the ceiling."

"David had to remove one seat," Heather explained. "But we can maneuver around it."

"He connected this to the fuel system?"

"Of course. How else could we—"

"That's much too dangerous."

"We talked about this months ago," Pat said.

"It's just a temporary alteration," Heather added.

"I don't think the owner would agree. How hard will it be to undo all this?"

"David says there's nothing to it. All he has to do is reinstall the missing seat and refit connections to the fuel system."

"He's tested it?"

"Whatever for? All it amounts to is a few connectors."

"You make it sound like the most natural thing in the world."

"Isn't it? Let me have Joe's leather jacket. It's in a puddle."

"What are you worried about, anyway?" Pat asked.

"I don't know."

"While you're deciding, let's get this over with."

As Pat and I handed up the luggage from the sodden pile, I noticed our own stuff was going in first. I asked Pat if that wasn't unfair.

"Not at all. In this mess, it's every man for himself, and they're both gone."

"I think some of this stuff should have been left in the cars. Joe can't want these maps of the Northwest Territory."

"When in doubt, pack."

Working silently, we handed everything up to Heather.

"That's it," Pat said. "I'm going to find Joe."

"Now that wasn't bad at all, was it?" Heather's head appeared over the mound of camping gear on the middle seat. "Although I must admit we're going to be a trifle tight in here."

"We'll have to make some adjustments when Joe gets back," I said. "But at least our belongings are out of the rain."

The belongings, not me. I was leaning into the cabin, my backside getting wetter by the minute as I shoved my boots behind the food carton. "Heather, we'd better clear the seats off."

"What a good idea. And where were you thinking of putting all this stuff? Look at all these books."

"Those are mine. They stay."

"And there are five jackets on this seat."

"We can hold those in our laps. Get the seatbelts free. Joe won't take off if we aren't buckled in, and this one's stuck under Pat's oxygen tank."

"I give up. Let's dump the lot on the food carton."

"It'll fall over."

She threw the jackets on top and pushed the shapeless mass. "It's not bad. The person in the middle can steady it against our plastic friend when the plane is at an angle."

"You're volunteering?"

"Why not. Anything else bothering you?"

"Yes. I think you're being much too casual. At least Joe has some sense. And by the way, maybe we should move the life raft oars. I don't think he'll want them under his feet."

"That's an interesting thought."

"Here, let me get them." I climbed onto the wing and opened Joe's door. It wasn't easy to pass the oars through the cabin, but we finally managed. Heather fussed around, trying them here and there.

"I think I've got it," she announced. "I'm going to try one on each side of the oxygen tank. There, that's done it. Quite a nice fit, actually."

"Will the life raft floorboards go alongside?"

"No, they're too long. And I don't see any other likely possibilities."

"To hell with it. Leave them on the back seat. We'll hold them in our laps. Let's go get something hot to drink."

But we were too late. Our friends were returning. "We've got it," Joe shouted, waving a piece of paper in my face.

"The flight plan?"

"Yes, and they brought, you know, a party. Here comes everybody."

I shivered. "Couldn't we have a quiet ceremony inside where it's dry?"

But no one answered. Ignoring the rain, our buddies served champagne, ginger ale, egg rolls and shrimp. The hor d'oeuvres were cool, but it was nine and we hadn't had anything to eat. I enjoyed the champagne toasts and was delighted that Joe was drinking ginger ale. So much for my pessimistic colleagues. I'd been hearing terrifying statistics about drunken private pilots for the last six months.

"Let's, you know, get this show on the road," Joe said.

"Don't you want to see how we packed the plane?" I asked.

He laughed and shook his head. And then we were surrounded by our friends. We hugged and kissed and shed a few tears before scrambling aboard to the pop of flashbulbs. Pat and I were in back with the unmanageable floorboards.

"What idiot put these on the seat?"

"This idiot. You have a better idea?"

After a brief experiment, we decided leaning against them was better than holding them. We settled back and struggled into our seatbelts, then turned to wave goodbye and blow kisses. I held my breath in anticipation.

3. The adventure begins

The great moment was slow in coming. Joe bent over the control panel with an impressive air of total concentration and turned the key. Nothing happened.

"What in blazes is going on?" He tried the ignition again.

"Maybe you flooded the engine," Pat suggested.

"Sounds the opposite to me," Joe replied.

"David, exactly what did you do to the fuel system?" I asked.

"Nothing. Adding that container changed nothing."

"But did you test it?" The engine refused to start. Joe slumped down in his seat with his head in his hands.

"No, I didn't test it. There was no need."

"Are you crazy? You're going to get us all killed—"

Joe tried the key again before exploding. "Useless, good-for-nothing fuel-injection engine!" When he failed to get a response on his next attempt, his curses shattered our eardrums.

Our friends were waiting in the rain. If we couldn't take off, we would have to undo the farewells, reload the cars, and drive up Tigertail Road to remove our notes from the mailboxes. I wasn't prepared to deal with immediate re-entry. I had been open with my friends, admitting how much I loved them. It had seemed important. We might not come back. But it would be humiliating not to leave.

"It must have started yesterday," Pat commented. "Joe flew the plane here from its home field."

"That was before David changed the fuel line. I think we should get a mechanic out here to—"

The roar of the engine stopped me. Joe's incantations had worked. The plane moved forward, then paused as he checked with the tower. We were on our way. I turned to look at our friends.

"They're jumping up and down like puppets," Heather said. "I had no idea they were so excited about the trip."

"They're glad to get rid of us." I blew kisses as the demonstration behind us expanded to include wild waving of arms and pointing. "You'd think they'd want to get out of the rain—"

I was interrupted by the controller's voice: "56 Whiskey, your cowl hatch is open."

"My God!" Pat groaned. "We put those sleeping bags in there and forgot to ask Joe to lock it."

"Jesus H. Christ!" David unbuckled his seat belt and followed Joe out the door.

They had just secured the hatch when Alan ran up. "Steve had to go inside to call the tower," he shouted. "Why did you ignore us?"

"Sorry about that." Joe solemnly shook his hand. "Thank the others for us. We'd have had that gear through the windshield over Anaheim if you hadn't noticed."

David and Joe settled into their seats. "No more nonsense!" Joe was upset. He called the tower, and, with slightly overdone assistance from that quarter, he taxied to the end of the runway.

We waited a long time for clearance. A small plane is airless in those moments before takeoff. Even short intervals seem interminable. I felt awful. I had just realized I was holding my breath when Joe looked back and shouted:

"Who can write fast? Gwen?"

"Anything you say."

"Write down everything you hear from now on."

I grabbed my notepad. "Talk slow."

Joe turned back to the controls as a disembodied voice said, "56 Whiskey cleared for takeoff."

"What do they mean, '56 Whiskey'?" I asked.

"That's the last part of the plane's registration number, 56W," Joe replied.

The engine roared and we were on our way. From my seat in back, it was hard to hear the radio. Certain that my life depended on it, I scribbled down every syllable I could decipher. The static was dreadful, but I did make out about half of a long string of numbers. Then, as Joe's conversation with the tower continued, I tried to record that, too.

Finally, all was silent. I expected Joe to ask for my notes. He didn't. After a few minutes, I screwed up my courage and yelled, "Joe, don't you want my notes?"

"What?"

"My notes." I held up the pad. "You asked me to take notes."

He stared at me for a moment, then shook his head and laughed so hard he almost choked.

"What's so damned funny?"

"You." He was still chuckling. "I didn't need any of that. They confirmed my instrument flight plan just as I filed it."

I was annoyed. But the exercise in futility had kept my mind off the takeoff, which wasn't all bad.

I settled back against the floorboards and looked out the window. We were gaining altitude rapidly, flying in the middle of a massive cloud bank. The clouds flowed through the cabin walls, as if they were permeable membranes.

"Pat, have you seen the clouds? Pat? Are you there?"

She didn't answer. She'd been using oxygen since we hit five thousand feet and was looking a trifle dazed. But she smiled a lot, so I wasn't concerned. I poked Heather's shoulder. "Look how the mist is swirling into the plane."

"That's not mist, silly. It's evaporation. Our clothes are drying out."

"But it's a cloud bank."

"We were pretty well soaked. Tell me, are you frightened?"

"You better believe it."

"So am I. But I wonder about David. He's shivering, and I can't tell if he's cold or scared."

"I say it's fear. Any normal human being would be scared."

"I suppose you're right. What about Joe? He must be upset about the plane being so overloaded. And then he had to take off in a storm—"

"Did you hear how he laughed at me? He's having the time of his life. Hey, we're coming out of the mist."

I sat back to enjoy the miracle. We were above the clouds, winging our way in the warmth of the sun toward Hermosillo. All of us were jubilant, especially Joe. He motioned toward the window and shouted, "We made it! Just look at this weather!" His dark brown eyes shone with delight.

"It's marvelous," I yelled back, feeling a vast relief. The worst was over. Now I could relax. The clouds below us parted, revealing gray slopes splashed with silvery light. I thought I recognized the hills near Irvine—a familiar landmark seen from another world.

As the cabin warmed up, we realized that David, who has sensitive, fair skin, was getting the sun right in the face. Heather and I scrambled through the luggage at our feet and found masking tape and a yellow bath towel. David taped the towel to the window on his right, and that helped a little. But he was still vulnerable to the sunlight streaming in the windshield. I offered him my yellow straw hat with purple ties. It looked foolish, but it would keep him from frying. David was on our minds, anyway. He had continued to sweat despite the cold rain. Since one of the intakes for the air circulation system was beside his seat, he was the only thing we could smell.

We crossed into Mexico under beautiful, clear skies. Before long, we had our first glimpse of the Sea of Cortez. The northern reaches were awe inspiring—brilliant turquoise water against soft beige sand. As we turned inland, the sea formed a watercolor backdrop of shimmering grays and blues, in cool contrast to the barren earth below. But the Sea of Cortez was a dream sea on a dream voyage. Far from intruding, its beauty enhanced my languor.

CHAPTER THREE
Mexico: Hermosillo to Los Mochis

1. Entering Mexico

Reality intruded when we landed at Hermosillo International Airport. It was a hot, dusty afternoon. We were in a foreign country, but it wasn't a fantasy land. It had a convincing solidity, a mundane quality, that stopped the dream. We stumbled out of the plane, and unreality came crashing back. Parked nearby, apparently ready to take to the air at any moment, was a World War II P-38. It seemed alien, discordant. I blinked several times, hoping it was a mirage.

We closed the plane and started toward the terminal. "God, I'm nervous," I said.

"What about?" Heather asked. "David and Joe have all the papers for the plane."

"I know, but I have to immigrate," I replied.

"You're worried about that? It's a cinch."

"For other people, yes. I'm the one who has the wrong papers. It happens every time. You'll all waltz on through, and there I'll be, trying to get the authorities to accept my visa."

"That's ridiculous."

"I can't help it," I said. "I hate red tape and being herded around like a prisoner—"

"Don't let them herd you around." Heather said. "Put them on the defensive. I think it'll be fun, don't you, David?"

"Piece of cake," he replied, steering us toward Immigration. "C'mon, Pat, Joe, let's get this over with."

We produced our papers, and two uniformed officers checked them over, then shook their heads. One of them made a long speech. None of us understood Spanish, but we read his gestures easily enough. We didn't have the right papers for the plane.

Heather glared at the official. "The Mexican Consulate in Beverly Hills gave us these papers. They must be right."

He shook his head. The papers were wrong. He held out his hand. "Twenty-five dollars." That part was in flawless English.

Pat, Joe and I were uncomfortable. We moved off while the argument continued. Finally David yelled, "Come on, gang. We're on our way."

"How much did that cost?" I asked as we headed back to the plane.

"Five dollars," David replied.

"How'd you manage that?"

"Persistence."

I wished I'd stuck around and listened. I might have learned something. But my distaste for confrontations was on a par with my feelings about red tape.

By the time Joe had filed his flight plan and we had gassed the plane, it was after three. "Isn't this a little late to be leaving?" I asked. "You said small planes weren't allowed to fly at night in Mexico."

"And I just found out there are no landing lights at Los Mochis," Joe agreed.

"Let's stay here," I suggested. "Everyone's exhausted."

"But our schedule—" Heather said. "We might have problems later on. We don't want to risk getting behind on the first day, do we?"

"O.K., O.K.. It doesn't matter to me. I can doze in back."

Soon we were on our way, flying toward the coast with dusk coming fast. Beneath us we could see nothing but a series of silvery sand bars leading to mud flats and, only distantly, to dry ground.

As the light faded, the mud flats became indistinguishable from the water. The sun, an immense orange disc, descended into an infinite sea. The last rays of light were beginning to disappear when the airstrip came into view. Relieved that we had made it, I listened casually as Joe called the tower.

"They're not answering. I don't get it. 56 Whiskey requesting permission to land—"

Joe tried several more times. We circled the airstrip as the sky darkened. In desperation, he decided to land without instructions. The sunset was gorgeous, but we hadn't planned on seeing it from the air.

We had just touched down when the radio came to life. It was the tower, and we could hear the controller loud and clear as he gave instructions to another plane. It was a by-the-book landing for that pilot, but listening to the conversation made us feel invisible.

The last sunlight had faded, and Joe turned on his lights before pulling into the parking area.

"Look," Heather said. "We're in luck. The parking lot is unpaved. We can sleep right here on the ground."

I turned in my seat and glared at her. "You're not thinking of camping out?"

"Why not? We have everything we need—a stove and food and—"

I was groping through my belongings, looking for my flashlight. "In case you didn't notice when we were circling, the Los Mochis Airport happens to be in the middle of a shanty town."

"No one's going to bother us."

"What makes you so sure? Anyway, it's so dusty I can taste it. If I had a flashlight, I'm sure I could see it. It's also God-damned dark."

"It's simply a matter of finding our flashlights."

"In this mess, I'll be lucky to find my shoes which, by the way, have been missing for the last hour."

"And I thought we had a dead rodent on our hands."

"Thank you, David."

"We're in business." Joe turned on his flashlight and opened his door.

"Well, we're all set to camp then," Heather said.

"No way. We're parked next to the runway."

"There won't be any more planes coming in tonight. We can sleep right here under the wing."

"We'd be totally unprotected. We're all exhausted. We need a good dinner and a night's sleep. Joe, tell her."

"Gwen's right. My back is turning into a pretzel. This is not the night to sleep on the ground."

"Can't take it, huh?" David asked. "In that case, I'll go hustle up a cab. Come on, Joe, you'd better tell the tower you exist."

David returned shortly to report his conversation with the owner of the plane that had followed us in. He had volunteered to send his cab back for us. And he had recommended the Santa

Anita Hotel. "Apparently the five of us can get a single large room for about fifteen dollars. And even I can afford that."

We laughed with relief. No one would have to feel guilty about forcing David to spend money he didn't have.

We waited for Joe and, in great spirits, climbed into a spring-less taxi for a bumpy ride into town.

2. *Lodging in Los Mochis*

Our luck ran out at the Santa Anita. We walked into the elegant lobby and several guests turned to stare. For the first time in hours, I looked at my buddies. We hadn't sorted ourselves when we left the plane, and we were a sight. Our non-drip-dry clothing had been sat dry, and no one had even tried to use a comb. My jeans were ancient, and my blue jacket was coming unglued at the seams. I had Pat's camera, complete with ten pound zoom lens, over my shoulder, and was carrying my overflowing nylon bag.

Heather was stunning in oversized khaki jacket and trousers and a pink chintz bonnet with a floppy ruffle that framed her large-boned features. I wanted to tell her she looked like a blue-eyed cocker spaniel passing for a little old lady, but decided against it.

Joe and Pat were well dressed by our standards, but they were so burdened with stuff bags, sloppy, misshapen bundles of books, and medical supplies that you couldn't tell.

Still, it was David who set the tone for the group. By this time he was preceded by his own locker-room stench. His heavy beard stubble was clearly not considered fashionable in Los Mochis, and my straw hat gave him a hippie look, accessorized as it was with an ancient, dirty knapsack, a camera, and the Sparklett's water bottle that he set on the counter. The water was a necessary constant companion in most of Mexico, but not in the lobby of the Santa Anita.

I was not surprised to hear that the price of a single room had escalated to thirty dollars. "What's the problem?" I asked. "I thought that pilot knew what he was talking about."

"David forgot to mention this is a mixed group," Joe said.

"No, I think it's us," Pat said. "I wouldn't rent a room to this motley crew."

I stood on one foot, feeling embarrassed and superfluous, while David and Heather argued with the desk clerk. When he refused to budge on the price, they gave up. Dragging our belongings after us, we retreated to the street.

"So now what?" Joe asked.

"Let's walk along and have a look at the town," Heather suggested.

Weighted down as we were, the going was slow. We were about a block down the road when she said, "Look, a travel agency. And they're open."

"But they won't speak English—"

I was too late. She and David were already inside, questioning the agent. They talked a long time before emerging with directions to a reasonably-priced hotel two blocks away.

The hotel staff was accommodating, although they were disturbed to learn that David and Heather would be sleeping together and she didn't have a wedding ring. I was annoyed that they considered it their business, which shows how naive I was about traveling in Latin countries.

"Why don't we register one room for the women and one for the men? They'll never know who is actually sleeping where," I said.

"It's a matter of principle," David replied.

We stepped back and waited for the argument to subside. And before long, Pat, Joe and I were stretched out on real beds. We rested for a while, then rotated through the cold shower, the first of many.

3. A surprising dinner

It was after nine when we finally rounded ourselves up for dinner. "How'd you like the cold shower?" I asked.

"What cold shower?" David replied. "We had hot water."

"How on earth?"

"Simple," Heather said. "You let the water run for thirty minutes before you get in."

"Now you tell me."

The street in front of the hotel was deserted. We moved slowly, our awkward gaits the result of kinky muscles.

"Tell me, Gwen, did you eat breakfast?" Joe asked.

"Sure. Don't you remember? Shrimp and caviar, wasn't it?"

"Egg rolls," David said. "And it wasn't breakfast."

"Hold this for a second." Pat handed me her purse and knelt to tie her shoelaces.

"Considering that lunch was a Coke, I call it breakfast."

"Fanta, Gwen, not Coke."

"I don't give a damn what they call it." Pat stood up. "I'm starving."

"I passed hunger somewhere over the Sea of Cortez," I said. "All I want is a beer."

"Cerveza," Pat said.

"How wonderful you've become so fluent."

"Gasolino is also a major part of my vocabulary. Hey, how about this? El Taquito it's called."

"Clean. Obviously cheap. And only two customers. It's perfect."

We ordered, in halting pseudo-Spanish, then sat staring at each other over our Dos Equis. The dining room smelled greasy, but our appetites revived when the cheese-covered enchiladas arrived. We downed them quickly, under the close scrutiny of a rather drunk member of the local scene. He was sitting at the next table, leaning over the back of his chair, leering at Heather, Pat and me.

Ignoring him, I turned to David. "So you and Joe met over a hot computer? You've worked together for years?"

"Since '67, to be exact. Joe's been in on all my projects."

"Computer projects?"

"Not for the most part. Although there were a few times, weren't there, old buddy? But the most fun we ever had was setting up my campus housing."

"Joe helped you decorate? Joe, why are you laughing?"

"He did, indeed. He not only picked out furniture, he delivered it."

"Meaning what? Where were you staying?"

"That was the difficult part. There wasn't room for me in the dorm, and I figured it was the university's responsibility to house me. So Joe and I did a little looking around and found an empty attic in the Engineering Building. That's where I lived."

"In the attic?"

"Yes. We selected furniture from various places around campus—a rug from theater arts, a chair from the green room in the music building. And by the time we were finished, it really looked quite spiffy."

"You stole furniture from campus buildings?"

"We borrowed it. When I moved out, we returned each and every item."

"How on earth—"

"You just roll the truck up and look official, and you can deliver anything. It was great sport."

"I don't know— Pat, had you heard any of this?"

"No. It's news to me."

"We've known you guys for a year. How come I never found out you are totally nuts?"

"Oh, that's all in the past," Joe said. "We've settled down."

Sleepy and replete, I accepted his assurance at face value. But I sat up straight when he said, "Yep, that was a real thrill, flying through the storm. I mean, it's one thing to understand instrument flying, but actually doing it is something else."

"Are you telling me you'd never flown on instruments before?"

"You got it. Never before today." He smiled. "I just passed the test three weeks ago. This was my first chance to try it out."

"Oh my God!"

"I thought it went very well."

"Sure, Joe, sure. You were great. It's just that— Oh, never mind. It's too late now—"

He laughed, shoulders shaking, enjoying my discomfort. I tried to laugh with him, but I felt queasy, as if I were at the top of a roller coaster about to take the plunge. This was going to be more of an adventure than I had imagined possible.

CHAPTER FOUR
Mexico: Los Mochis to Acapulco

1. A leisurely breakfast

I was rudely awakened at the crack of dawn by the glorious morning greeting of a rooster crowing at the foot of my bed. I opened my eyes and was surprised to discover he was nowhere to be seen. Stumbling up, I found the window and leaned out. There he was, in the central courtyard three stories below, strutting about, then pausing for another guttural yodel. He was clearly pleased by the thunderous megaphone effect his song produced as it ricocheted back and forth off the courtyard walls. This was undoubtedly his favorite spot. Or perhaps the management had hired him to enforce early checkout.

In any case, I was wide awake and assumed Pat and Joe must be, too. That was my first mistake. A quick glance told the whole story: they were avoiding morning at all cost. Both had burrowed deep under their covers.

Convinced that the crowing must have awakened them, I launched into a monologue. "Let's see. It's nine now, so by the time we have breakfast and get to the airport, it'll be after eleven. And then Joe has to file his flight plan—"

"Nine? Are you serious? We'll never make Acapulco." Pat was out of bed and throwing on her clothes. "But wait. My watch shows quarter to six."

"How strange. Mine must be fast. Now what are we going to do about this aardvark here?"

"Well, he did warn us that he's nocturnal."

"I know all about it. I've tried to call him in the morning several times. Apparently he's in the habit of sleeping until noon. But wouldn't you think he'd get up on a great trip like this?"

"He knows we can't leave without him. We may end up holding a vigil around his bed."

"Nonsense. There has to be a better way. I'm going for reinforcements."

David and Heather were on the other side of the hotel, which meant they had been without benefit of a wakeup rooster. I stood at their door, banging and shouting, for a long time before Heather appeared. I was surprised to see that she had slept in her chintz cap. It was oddly discordant with her white long johns.

"You've got to come help me. Joe is refusing to wake up, and we're going to be stuck in Los Mochis forever."

"That does present something of a problem, doesn't it? We'll be there in ten minutes."

"Make that fifteen," David shouted.

"Five or I'm gone," I said, retracing my steps. This kind of waiting was maddening for a morning person like me. Besides, I wanted my coffee. But this group wasn't to be hurried. It was thirty minutes before we started off for breakfast, by which time I felt as if I'd put in a full day's aggravation.

Seeing Los Mochis in daylight was a shock. With all it's neons blazing, it had appeared larger and more prosperous. In fact, it is a lazy, dusty town, hemmed in by agriculture and poverty. Still, the early air felt new and fresh, and the warmth from the sun was soft.

"Where to, folks?" I asked.

"Let's eat at the Santa Anita," Heather suggested. "If it's so classy, they must serve a good breakfast."

"But will they let us in?" I wasn't eager to make a fool of myself again.

"Why wouldn't they? Aren't you curious about it?"

The subdued elegance of the dining room reminded me that this was not a place to approach with a Sparklett's water bottle in hand. I was surprised when they seated us, but then, most of their guests were still sleeping.

We served ourselves from the lavish buffet, sticking for the most part to bacon and eggs. David had his usual three or four helpings of everything, and the rest of us watched him eat with awe.

2. Interior decorating

Fortified, and in much better humor, we collected our belongings and caught a cab to the airport. David and Joe busied themselves with gas and oxygen, filing the flight plan, checking weather, and the other necessary formalities.

Having nothing else to do, the rest of us carried our gear back to the plane. Pat and I were cramming everything inside when Heather said, "I have an idea. While they're busy with all that paper work, why don't we repack the plane?"

"Why don't we pretend you didn't say that?" I continued shoving our bundles behind the seats.

"But don't you see? We'll be much more comfortable if we get things sorted out properly."

"What I see is that we'll have to unload everything. That will take at least an hour, and our stuff will get filthy in this dust.

What if you can't get it all back in? Have you thought of that? We brought too much, in case you hadn't noticed."

"All the more reason to repack it."

"O.K., go ahead, but I'm not helping. It's a lousy idea."

"You're taking this much too seriously. I have a plan."

With Pat's assistance and only a minor delay in departure, Heather succeeded in completely restructuring our environment. I grudgingly admitted it was a vast improvement and, as a form of peace offering, I moved up to the stewardess seat in the middle. Heather and Pat were now in back, but they were much more comfortable. Heather had cleverly stowed the life raft boards against the wall on the doorless side of the plane.

"Heather," I yelled over the roar of the engine, "I take it all back. It's only ten o'clock, and you've found a place for everything. You're a total genius."

Her bonnet, which she had taken to wearing in the cabin, shook as she laughed. "It is better, isn't it?"

3. My new duties

My offer to change places with Heather was more generous than I had realized. As occupant of the middle seat, I was in charge of passing everything from water and cookies to communications. I didn't mind playing stewardess, but the roar of the engine made passing the messages tough.

It usually started with Heather poking my shoulder. She would point down and shout: "Ask David the name of that river."

I would poke David, point, and shout: "Heather wants to know the name of that river."

David would peer out the window, fumble with the gigantic map he kept in his lap, hold it up to show us the spot, and shout, "It's the (blank) river."

Me: "It's the (blank) river."

Heather: "What?"

By this time, David would have turned around. Reading Heather's lips, he would bellow: "(blank)."

Heather: "Have you taken a picture?"

Me: "Have you taken a picture?"

David: "A picture? Jesus Christ, no! Joe, pull a circle on that river."

Joe would smile and turn the plane around, dipping first one wing, then the other. Finally, our photo taking complete, David would hand me the map so that each of us could view (blank) in its proper geographic perspective. Much as I love water, I came to dread the next sighting.

But I was beginning to appreciate the flexibility we had, traveling in a private plane. We could follow a river on a whim, or turn out toward the coast for a look around. And, between rivers, I could read, write, fantasize or doze. Joe was being the perfect professional, totally involved in his work. Whatever other odd ideas he might have, he took his flying seriously.

David did, too. He was studying his maps and following Joe's work with the instruments. Pat was deeply immersed in a book. Heather looked miserable. She suffers from air sickness, and we had taken one too many turns around the (blank) river.

As we neared the coast, the character of the land changed abruptly. We had been flying over arid or irrigated flat lands relieved by milk chocolate mountains. Now we were looking down on the lush, undifferentiated green of a tropical jungle. Seen from above, it was as unlikely as a movie set. We had reached this wild country quickly, and would as soon be gone.

"What's that town down there?" Heather asked.

Me: "What's that town?"

David: "Mazatlan. Look at that incredible bay."

Heather: "Joe, can we fly around it?"

Me: "Joe, Heather wants to fly around the city."

"What? Around Mazatlan?" He grinned and turned the plane into a wide bank. The view of the sprawling town and its elegant bay crowned with granite cliffs took my breath away.

About an hour below Mazatlan, Pat spotted a vast swamp just behind the coast. We went exploring. The swamp stretched on endlessly, a billowing sea of iridescent greens. White egrets, the embodiment of grace, glided above. We soared higher still in our Great Bird of the Swamp, circling over the mangroves, the rolling grasses, the green slime.

"What's that in the middle?" Pat asked.

"Looks like a town," Heather said. "A circular town. How astonishing."

"They must have built it around that enormous church."

"That's all very well," I said, "but how do people get in and out? Heather, can you see any roads on your side?"

"No," Heather replied. "And it would be tough getting a boat through those mangroves."

"But it's there, well-built, prosperous— There has to be a way in!"

We circled several more times and left reluctantly, our curiosity unsatisfied.

4. Puerto Vallarta to Acapulco

The Puerto Vallarta airport was ablaze with flowers. Joe parked and we scrambled out. Joe and David went off to find the tower. We went in search of the restrooms. Eventually we regrouped with Fantas, our standard lunch, in hand. Joe taxied to the gas pump and soon we were back in our own private world.

The rocky, precipitous coastline between Puerto Vallarta and Acapulco is an unending sequence of dark blue sea, emerald bays, and steep granite cliffs, set against luxuriant green hills and dazzling blue sky. It seemed excessive. I longed for an occasional barren desert, a brown hillside, a misplaced rock.

But even hours of repetitive perfection did not dull the impact of my first sight of Acapulco. The bay must be among the loveliest in the world. Cliffs rise on each side, framing the nearly symmetrical beach and its phalanx of towering rocks. It is a perfectly executed design grand enough to have been the playground of the gods. We circled several times before landing.

I was climbing down over the wing when Joe said, "David's gone to find the tanker truck."

"I thought you weren't worried about the gas shortage."

"I'm not worried. I just sleep better on a full tank."

"My God!" Pat said. "Here they come now. Snap your fingers and the gas truck pulls up."

Joe laughed. "See that, Gwen? Your friends are a bunch of worrywarts."

Pleased with our efficiency, we then spent two hours haggling. Heather and David wanted to rent a car and find a camping site. Joe, Pat and I were in favor of taking a cab to the nearest hotel.

But we couldn't even agree on how much money to change to pesos, or the correct translation for "Where is the ladies' room?"

Finally, Joe said, "Enough already. We're going to take a cab into town." Heather had to sit on David's lap in the front seat, but he didn't object. The driver found us a comfortable, reasonably-priced motel and we collapsed.

5. The ugly Americans

Around seven, we joined David and Heather. It was still quite warm. The water looked inviting, so we opted for a stroll along the beach before dinner. But we soon discovered open sewers draining directly into the exquisite bay. The smell was appalling, and we couldn't get away from it. In desperation, we held our noses and followed one of the sewers down the middle of the street all the way back to the main drag.

"Jesus H. Christ, what a God-awful mess!" David said.

"We stumbled off the set." Exhausted from the walk, Pat sat down on a bench.

We tried to laugh the mood away, but it hurt to realize that the beauty of Acapulco was a sham.

"So what now?" Joe asked. "Anyone ready to eat?"

"I am always ready to eat," David said.

"Let's find a cab," I suggested. "Pat's tired."

"Don't be ridiculous. I can walk."

"I have an idea." Heather tugged at her chintz bonnet. "There's a fancy hotel two blocks down the road. Let's go there."

"Not the Hyatt Regency?"

"That's the one. They must serve good food there, don't you think? And we need cheering up."

We had not changed from our ancient khakis and jeans—
there being nothing to change into—so I argued for something
less elegant. But David and Heather were adamant, and I was
learning.

In the ornate lobby, we perused the posted menus for the
many eating places in the hotel.

"These look a little steep," I said. "Let's go back to the city."

"I feel like a good dinner," David replied.

"But you're always looking for a cheap place to eat—"
I protested.

"I say," Heather beckoned us over. "This menu is fantastic.
And it's a formal dining room on the roof. The view must be
spectacular."

"Perfect." David started toward the elevator.

"They'd never let us in," Pat said.

"Sure they would. You just have to be firm. Come on, we'll
show you how it's done—"

"I believe you. But are you prepared to pay ten bucks for
your vegetables?"

"Ten bucks?" David squinted at the small print.

The dining room they finally settled on wasn't fancy, but
we were still a trifle underdressed. Fortunately, the waiters took
us for eccentrics. They treated us with respect, and even laughed
uproariously when Heather asked to sample five different cakes
on the dessert wagon before making a selection.

I wasn't so easily amused. I felt like an ugly American—
speaking only English, dressing outrageously, talking loudly,
demanding my rights, under-tipping. But I was no match for
David and Heather. They were the experts.

As we straggled out of the dining room, I tried to lead the way toward the entrance. Heather stopped me.

"Let's go see the roof." She gave me a push toward the elevator. "The view must be sensational, and the most they can do is throw us out."

"We can't go up there looking like this," I protested.

"Don't be silly," David said. "What's so important about clothes? Anyway, we're not going to stay long."

"Besides, it's high time you learned how to get along in the world." Heather pushed the call button.

An elegantly dressed couple got in at the third floor. They pressed themselves far back into the corner, ignoring us.

"Damn!" Pat said.

"What's the matter?"

"I forgot to tell Alan not to feed the pregnant rat to the snake."

"Don't you think he'll figure that out for himself?"

"How do you identify a pregnant rat?"

We reached the roof and the couple fled. Laughing, we stepped into another ornate lobby. "What are you going to do?" I was feeling decidedly uncomfortable.

"Walk in. What else?" Heather's eyebrows arched with amazement at my innocence.

Joe, Pat and I cringed against the wall as they swept past the maitre d' and onto the terrace. We did our best to fade into the woodwork. The minutes dragged by. Finally, they reappeared.

"You guys really missed it. You could be standing at the door to Fort Knox and you wouldn't know what to do," David said.

"Right on." Joe's shoulders shook with laughter.

We assaulted the gift shops before making our way back to the motel.

6. Breakfast in Acapulco

It was five a.m. when Heather appeared at our door. She was wearing her white longies, but, to my great disappointment, had taken her cap off. We had a whispered conference about where to eat breakfast.

"There won't be anything open at the airport, not at this hour," she said.

"Let's eat in town, then," I suggested. "I don't want to starve all day."

"We can walk until we find a restaurant," Pat suggested.

"Are you sure you can manage?" Heather asked. "You were pretty tired last night."

"I'm fine. There's no need to call a cab."

We all moved quickly, for once, and within a few minutes we were ready. We picked up our disorganized luggage, threw it over our shoulders, and started out the rear exit of the motel.

I suppose our behavior looked suspicious. The night watchman thought so, anyway. He came running after us, shaking his fist and shouting in Spanish. We couldn't understand what he was saying, but it was clear that he wanted proof that we had paid our bill. Unfortunately, I was the one who had taken care of it. I had a terrible time locating the receipt. It was still dark, and he stood next to me, shouting in my ear as I fumbled through my purse. In desperation, I emptied my stuff bag on the ground and, with the aid of a flashlight, found the crumpled paper. Grumpily, he allowed us to move on.

"My God, I'm a wreck," I said to Heather.

"Really? Why is that? David and I think it would be fun to return to the Regency for breakfast. Would you like that?"

"Just what I need," I mumbled.

We must have been a remarkable sight, filing up that elaborate staircase in our ragged attire, weighed down by our motley assortment of bags. My nerve almost failed me, but David and Heather were plowing ahead, and Joe and Pat were following with resolute lack of concern.

We trudged into the dining room, piled our belongings in front of the waterfall next to the window, and settled into the deep chairs.

"The place is almost deserted," Heather commented.

"There are some people over there." Joe waved toward the opposite side of the room.

"In case you didn't notice," I said, "there was a smartly dressed couple at the next table when we came in. They got up and left."

"Probably finished," David said.

"They left their plates untouched," I replied.

"Then they remembered an appointment," Pat said. "There's no point in being paranoid."

David ate his usual phenomenal amount—sausage, eggs, toast, potatoes, cereal, fruit. He was in a great mood and offered to pay. I knew that was a mistake. When David paid, there was always trouble. This time, we were followed down the hall by the distressed maitre d'. He was particularly vociferous, but David persuaded him that the traveler's checks were good, and we were allowed to leave.

Heather discovered the spacious lounges near the lobby, and everyone decided to have a good wash. We had planned to rendezvous on the front steps in preparation for making the decision to hire a cab. The process took a while because one or another member of the group kept disappearing to buy postcards or Kleenex. In the meantime, we had taken over the steps and were interfering with the egress rights of the early morning tennis players. But by now I was feeling quite in touch with my own rights in the world, and I didn't move to make it easier for them. I could see that this trip was going to change us all, and wasn't sure it would be for the better.

It was nine when we reached the airport. Everyone disappeared on the usual uncoordinated errands, leaving me to guard the plane. When Pat returned, I left her in charge and ran the length of the field to the main terminal. I was determined to find a straw hat for David. He was wearing mine everywhere, and I suspected I'd never get it back. But I returned empty handed.

We refilled our plastic water bottles from the drinking fountain, Joe checked the weather and filed his flight plan, and then we were on our way to Tapachula, our exit point from Mexico.

CHAPTER FIVE
Tapachula, Mexico to Managua, Nicaragua

1. Volcano Corridor

Tapachula International was an easy stop. There were no other customers. We had our passports stamped, then stretched out on the grass while Joe and David filed the flight plan. I was content to lie in the sun, but Heather and Pat were restless. They went looking for something to photograph, and had just discovered an enormous black bug, when Joe called us.

"What's for lunch?" he asked. I handed him a Fanta. "So let's go, already. We have several hours of flying ahead."

"Don't we need gas?" Pat was reluctant to leave her bug.

"We filled up. We still haven't found your gas shortage, Gwen."

"Mea culpa. Can we forget it now?" We strolled across the grass and boarded the plane.

"Seatbelts on?" Joe asked. We assured him they were. He spoke briefly to the tower, then taxied down the dirt airstrip. Soon we were above Tapachula, heading into a tall stack of white cumulus clouds. The cozy cotton wool world was hypnotic, and I drifted into a deep sleep.

I awoke with a start. Joe was shaking my knee. "Hello in there!"

"Good morning, Joe. You can let go of my knee now."

"I had to get your attention."

"Why?"

"We're out of the storm. You were about to miss Central America."

"Which part?"

"El Salvador. You slept through Guatemala."

"Damn. Why didn't you wake me?"

Joe laughed. "Shut up and look."

We had seen so much of beauty in the past few days, I didn't expect to react. But the green, rolling hills set against a distant backdrop of smoking volcanos and a sky as clear as a polished mirror were riveting. I realized I was hearing music in my head, the music that had been missing for so many months. It was Chopin, his first Ballade. Elation flowed through me like a current. I was happy.

I stared at the countryside until my eyes ached, then settled back. The plane was great, Joe was a bona fide professional, and Heather's planning was paying off. What a marvelous trip!

My serenity was shattered by a deafening silence. The engine had stopped. I struggled upright as Joe tried the ignition. The engine sputtered but didn't catch. Looking out at the landscape that only a moment before had seemed so peaceful, I wondered how it would feel to be part of it. And then Joe tried the ignition once more. I held my breath as the engine sputtered, sputtered again, then caught. It was over, the ghastly silence vanquished.

I expected Joe to turn and explain. When he didn't, I poked his shoulder. "What was that all about?"

"What was what all about?"

"My God, Joe, don't tell me you didn't notice the engine stopped."

"Oh that."

"Is it O.K.?"

He shrugged. "It started."

"That's not good enough. What do you know about the history of this plane?"

"The plane's fine. I forgot to switch gas tanks. We ran out of gas on one, and I restarted on another tank. That's it."

"But I—"

"But you what?"

"Never mind. You guys and your nerves of steel."

"Would you feel better if I had hysterics?" Joe's eyes twinkled.

"Just don't do it again," I snapped.

Shaken, I paid close attention as Joe maneuvered the plane parallel to the shore. Waves lapped at the beach, white foam spreading backward onto the water and forward onto the sand. Behind the verdant foothills, clusters of cloud-shrouded volcanos marched inland, whispering ominous threats.

And then Joe turned left. It was a few minutes before I realized what that meant. "Damn it, Joe," I yelled. "You're headed for Nicaragua."

"Right again!"

"We agreed to avoid Managua. Don't you remember that article? The one about Americans not being welcome—"

"A wild exaggeration," David replied. "That magazine was two years old. We won't have any trouble now."

"But my friends told me—"

"Your gas shortage friends?" Joe was laughing.

"You have a point."

"The only alternative is Panama, and Managua's closer. Besides, I've already filed my flight plan."

"Well, you could have asked—"

"In case you've forgotten, I'm the pilot."

"Carry on, Captain." I saluted and sank back into my seat. He was taking all the responsibility. The least I could do was shut up.

2. Managua

It was a beautiful flight inland, and I soon forgot my misgivings. A routine landing added to my sense of security. I climbed out, thinking about finding a hotel and a hot bath. From the runway, the terminal building looked inviting. Reflection pools decked with flowers enhanced its serene, spacious appearance. But the exterior walls were covered with scaffolding, a remodeling project so extensive that it jarred. I was wondering about this when Heather poked my shoulder. "Now what do you suppose they want?"

"Who?"

"Those unpleasant looking men in uniform."

"I'll be damned! Our own reception committee. Joe, did you request a limo?"

Our banter stopped when the officials confronted us. "Il piloto?" the leader looked at Joe and David.

"I'm the pilot," Joe replied.

"Papers." Joe pulled the flight plan from his pocket and handed it over. "Tapachula."

"Sí, Tapachula."

The officer studied Joe for a moment, then said, "Come with us."

"But we aren't organized—" Joe replied.

"Come with us."

They surrounded us like prisoners and marched us inside. Someone handed us immigration forms.

"What's going on?" I whispered to David.

"You're supposed to fill out the form."

"Thanks a lot." My hand was shaking, but I managed to get my passport number right. We handed the completed forms to an unsmiling fat man.

"This way." The leader started off.

"Where are you taking us?" Heather demanded.

No answer. They led us back to the plane.

"This is perfectly ridiculous—"

The leader interrupted Heather midstream. "Get your luggage. Take what you need."

"Could you give us a few minutes?" Joe asked. "We want to get gas before we leave the airport—"

"Impossible. No gasolino."

"No gas— But—"

"No gasolino. Get your luggage."

The five of them surrounded the plane. We gathered stuff bags and cameras, and Joe locked the doors. Without a word, they herded us back to the main terminal building and through the immigration hall. The man in charge opened the door of a small room and pointed inside. We filed in, and two of the officials followed. They closed the door and stood against it. One of them motioned to us to sit down.

An uncharacteristic hush fell over us. The only sound was the squeaking of the red plastic chairs as we squirmed to ease our backaches. Time seemed to stand still.

"I told you we shouldn't come here, David," I whispered.

"Cut the crap."

"We need a plan," Pat said.

Joe leaned forward and looked at Pat. "A plan for what? We don't even know what's happening."

"We must have done something wrong." Heather's voice was higher than usual.

"We did. We came here," Pat replied.

"I know what it is," I said. "We smell."

David snorted. "We don't smell."

"I may be wrong about me, but I'll tell you something, David. You do smell. And you have since Santa Monica."

"Keep your voice down." Joe sounded frightened. "Maybe they think we're smuggling drugs."

"Don't even say that word," Pat cautioned.

"David, it's the visas," Heather said. "There's something wrong with our visas."

"That's impossible. They haven't asked for the passports yet."

As if on cue, a tall, skinny official entered the room and held out his hand. "Passports."

We handed them over. He stowed our collective identities in his pocket and walked out without another word.

"I feel anonymous," Pat said.

"It must be my vibes," Joe commented. "I feel like that a lot." He shrugged, but he wasn't laughing.

David was thumbing through his wallet, looking subdued. "Heather, you're the one who's traveled all over the world. What did you do when something like this happened?"

"Nothing like this has ever happened to me."

The door opened and an official we hadn't seen before came in and beckoned us to follow him.

"Now what?" Heather asked.

"The firing squad, no doubt," I replied. He stopped beside a table in the large, nearly empty immigration hall, and told us to set our bags down. Then he motioned to the others to move on.

When I started to follow, he held out his arm and pointed to the bags.

"Me?" I asked. His reply was in Spanish. He gave an order and pointed at me. One of the guards came and stood over me as the leader marched my friends to the other side of the room and up a flight of stairs. My guard moved to the doorway.

I sat on the edge of the table and pulled out a book. I thought it would be better to look busy. But I couldn't read. I was alone— and frightened. If only we knew what was wrong. We had landed normally enough. But that was when it had started.

It must have been Joe. He must have broken some rule or other. Or perhaps it was the plane. Maybe it fit the description of some drug dealer's plane. Our papers were gone, we were separated, we were prisoners— Maybe they thought we were spies. We would be rotting in jail and no one would know where to look for us.

That was it! A letter! It was up to me to get word out. I would write to Alan. I found an unused postcard from Acapulco and wrote a hasty note:

Hi Alan—

Not sure what's going on, but if we don't turn

up on time, look for us in Managua.

Love to all— Gwen

That should get his attention. Oh God, the only stamps in my purse were Mexican. I looked around the room. A thin young man was lounging against the far wall, watching me. I smiled at him and waved. Out of the corner of my eye, I could see the guard lighting a cigarette.

The young man slunk over. "Buenas días."

"Buenas días," I replied. "¿Habla usted inglés?"

"No. ¿Habla usted español?"

"No. Es necessario— ¿Stamps— er, estampas?" I pointed at the postcard and held out a five dollar bill. He laughed and reached for the money. "No. Estampas," I gave him a one dollar bill, "then this," I waved the bribe. I handed over the postcard and the dollar and watched him round the corner. I was afraid the guard would intervene, but he appeared not to have noticed.

Eager to see what my friend was doing, I started across the room. A large hand grabbed my shoulder. I turned and smiled at the guard.

"¿Dondé está el lavabo de mano?" I was pretty sure that was the right way to ask for the rest room. We'd worked on that one.

"No. You go there." He pointed at the luggage.

"But— "

He took my elbow and escorted me back to my seat. It wasn't long before the messenger returned. He was all smiles. My hand shook as I gave him his reward, but the guard was ignoring us. I wished I could be sure he hadn't filed the card in the nearest trash container.

I pulled out my book. I could feel the young man staring at me. He probably wanted another fiver. I pretended to be reading. He continued to stare. Finally, I heard the others coming down the stairs. Relief flooded through me at the sight of them.

"What happened? Where have you been?"

"Upstairs." Heather gestured toward the second floor. "Joe and David were being interrogated, and I didn't know what was going on."

David shook his head. "I still don't know."

"I thought you guys would never come down," Pat said.

"Where were you?" I asked.

"I couldn't manage the stairs. The guard made me wait on the first landing."

I grabbed Joe's arm. "Is it all right? Are we being detained?"

"I think everything's all right now, but I'm not sure."

"Didn't they explain?"

"Their English wasn't great," David said. "They questioned us about who we were and where we'd been—"

"And then this guy we'd never seen before comes in and gives us the passports—here's yours, by the way—and everybody starts talking about gas."

"Gas? As in shortage?"

"Yes. We can't get any. Private planes are not allowed to purchase gas under any circumstances."

I laughed. "So it's not non-existent after all."

"This isn't a joke," David said. "That scene up there was a long way from funny."

"Well, it wasn't exactly comedy hour down here."

The guard motioned us forward. Soberly, we waited while our luggage was inspected. My young friend had been lurking behind the officials. Now he carried our bags out to the street and dumped them in front of the waiting cabs. Joe tipped him handsomely.

"So cheer up, gang," I said. "We've immigrated, and we're free to go wherever we choose."

"Except on with our trip," Joe replied.

"I want to get to the bottom of this." Heather wet her lips. "Let's go find the Airport Manager."

"Good thinking," Joe agreed. "Gwen, Pat, you stay with the gear."

We made ourselves comfortable on the stuff bags.

"Buenas días." It was my friend again.

"Buenas días," I replied. The taxi drivers, who were waiting like vultures in front of their ancient vehicles, cracked up.

"¿Más estampes?" he asked.

I shook my head. Forever the ham, I searched my memory for the sparse remnants of my one semester Spanish course. I tried again. "¿Cómo se llama usted?"

"Carlos." Then he mumbled something I couldn't understand.

I shook my head. All I remembered were the numbers. "Uno, dos, tres—"

With, I thought, the best will in the world, Carlos began reciting phrases which I tried to repeat. The cab drivers were amused. But then, my pronunciation is always greeted with hysteria whether it's German, Swahili, or French. Why should Spanish be any different? After a while, he asked me in halting English where we were going.

"Managua," I replied.

"Managua, no." Carlos gestured with his hands as he told me in Spanish what was wrong with the city.

"Did you hear that, Pat? What do you think he's saying?"

"I have no idea." She returned to her book.

Carlos tried again. I missed most of what he said, but one point was clear. "He says this airport is between two cities, and we should go to the other one. It's called Tipitapa."

"Sure," Pat mumbled.

"Tipitapa," Carlos nodded. "You go La Mercedes."

"La Mercedes?" I repeated as the drivers roared.

"Sí, La Mercedes. You go there."

"He suggested a hotel, Pat, isn't that nice? La Mercedes in Tipitapa."

"And I suggest you stop talking to him."

"Such a cynic. Here they come. I think the news is bad."

"We are getting nowhere fast," Joe said. "Let's find a hotel. I can't take much more of this."

"I've had a great time. Carlos has been telling me about a hotel in Tipitapa. He says we should go there—"

Joe put up his hand. "This is no time to play tourist. All I want is a nice, comfortable room in a simple Managua hotel."

"Managua it is."

3. A simple Managua hotel

When we picked up our gear, we were surrounded by the cab drivers. David elbowed a path to the nearest vehicle. We climbed in carefully, having learned in Mexico that the seats would be hard and lumpy. Joe, Pat and I were jammed in the back, Heather and David in front.

"Let's get out of here." Joe was leaning forward as if he could will the cab away from the airport.

"Wait!" Heather pulled her out-of-date Auto Club guide from her purse. "We need the name of a hotel. How about the Hilton? I want to be pampered."

"She's right," Pat said. "It's after seven, and we're all tired."

The driver turned onto a tree-lined highway. At the first bump, it became clear that the cab had no springs. It was going to be a slow ride into town.

"Oh my God! No wonder." Pat pointed to a vast heap of rubble beside the road.

"No wonder what?" I asked.

"The earthquake. A year ago, Managua had a horrendous earthquake."

"The news was full of it. The city's in ruins," Heather said. "How could we have forgotten?"

"We had a few other things on our minds," Joe replied.

Rickety shacks dotted the vivid green landscape. A decrepit bus, packed with people, labored up the hill ahead of us, protesting each shift of the gears with belches of oily exhaust. As we approached the city, the piles of rubble rose higher and higher, reminding us that Managua had been at the epicenter of the earthquake.

The driver slowed to merge with a continuous stream of ancient cars, donkeys, and thin, weary people clad in bright tatters. Many pushed handcarts or carried awkward bundles. I didn't want to be there, staring at them. But David and Joe were eager to capture the scene on film. Several times they ordered the driver to stop so that they could set up their shots. I felt ashamed, self-important in a taxi, watching with tourist detachment this struggle for survival.

I was relieved when we reached the hotel. David and Heather went to the desk. We walked to the edge of the parking lot and looked out. A beautiful modern building, the Hilton normally commands a spectacular view of the business district and of Lake Managua far below. But the hotel was one of the few structures still standing in the central section of the city. The rest had been reduced to the pile of rubble that was strewn all the way down to the lake. It was a frightening spectacle.

"You can see why they keep rebuilding here," Pat commented. "Just look at that lake. I'd take a big risk to have that view."

"I'd like a closer look at the damage pattern," Joe said. "I'll do an overflight tomorrow. We should be able to see the whole thing."

Heather and David joined us. "That's an amazing sight," she commented.

"It makes you feel insignificant, doesn't it?" Pat replied.

"What did you find out?"

"There aren't any rooms. I can't imagine what we were thinking. There has to be a shortage of accommodations in a disaster area."

"So find us another hotel, Heather." Joe opened the cab door for us.

"Why don't we camp out?" I asked.

"Camp out?" David turned to stare at me. "Why would we do that?"

"I've been asking that question for a week now. If we're ever going to do it, this would be a perfect spot. There are lots of people sleeping out here every night."

"We're tired," Joe said. "We need a good rest."

We waited while Heather read hotel names from her book. The driver didn't reply. He simply raised and lowered his hands at the mention of each, to indicate that it, too, had crumbled to the ground. Finally, in broken English, he suggested a small pension nearby.

"It sounds marvelous!" Heather exclaimed.

The old house looked inviting, but it, too, was full. The manager suggested another small hotel that might have rooms.

We drove for ten or fifteen minutes, finally stopping in front of what was obviously a private home turned into rooms-to-let. The proprietor, a grossly fat German, sat at a desk near the front door. He seemed inanimate, like a large piece of furniture. He glared at us coldly through thick glasses suggestive of monocles.

"Single rooms, yes. Down the stairs, to your left. Numbers six through ten."

A quick inspection was discouraging. The rooms were cramped and dirty.

"It's too late to be choosy." David led the way back to the desk. But he changed his mind when the proprietor asked for thirty dollars each.

"That's ridiculous," Heather said. "Gwen, how about that hotel in Tipitapa? The one your airport friend mentioned. Let's call them."

David grabbed the phone book on the desk. "Yeah. What was the name?"

Like a trained parrot, I repeated, "La Mercedes."

The German, who had followed our conversation closely, roared with laughter. "That's a whore house."

No wonder the drivers were so amused.

We beat a hasty retreat to the cab. Our driver seemed sympathetic. He shook his finger under my nose. "La Mercedes, por usted, mala." It was comforting that he felt that way.

He hailed a passing cab to ask for suggestions, and we were off again in hot pursuit of a place to stay.

For some reason, this address was almost impossible to find.

When we passed the same corner for the third time, I was sure we were lost. "Tell me again why tonight, of all nights, we have to find rooms. We could go back to the airport and sleep on the couches."

"There aren't any," David pointed out.

"Well, the chairs then. Comfort is not normally your chief concern."

"We don't normally get the shit scared out of us," David replied.

I had to admit the events of the afternoon had been frightening. But I'd been equally frightened every other day. I decided it was a new experience for the others.

The driver turned onto a small winding street where little earthquake damage was in evidence, and stopped in front of an old, red-tiled mansion surrounded by lush gardens. It had been beautiful at one time.

Heather, David and our driver disappeared into the garden, searching for the entry. They were gone a long time, and I was falling asleep when they burst upon us.

"We have great rooms," David said.

"Hallelujah!" I grabbed my bag and jumped out.

"It's quite nice," Heather agreed. "It's run by a German woman, and German's the one language I really know."

"You didn't use it at the last place," I said.

"It would have been a waste of breath. But we need it here. She translated for me. I arranged for our driver to pick us up in the morning."

We were shown to small, clean rooms. There were two large bathrooms with showers. Meals were included and, even though it was after ten, the owner had agreed to feed us. We were all feeling lightheaded. We had eaten breakfast in Acapulco at seven, and drunk Fantas in Tapachula. That had been it. And we had burned up a lot of energy sitting around Immigration. We weren't out of trouble yet, but the prospect of dinner raised our spirits.

The table was pleasantly set, and we felt festive. The proprietress, a sweet-faced woman in blue, brought out small glasses of cold fruit juice.

"My God! This is the best drink I've ever had," David said. "What is it?"

"The syrup from a can of apricots," Heather replied.

Pat held her glass up to the light. "No, it's the nectar of the gods."

"I don't suppose you might be a little dehydrated." Heather spoke briefly to our hostess. "She's bringing some more."

Pat's face lighted up, and she smiled ruefully. "It's humiliating to want apricot syrup so much."

We let her have most of the juice.

After dinner, we retired to Joe's tiny quarters for a strategy meeting. Joe's shoulders were stiffer than ever, and I massaged his back while the others studied the maps. The room was crowded, but cozy. Everyone seemed in a much better mood as we discussed the topics uppermost in our minds: painful shoulder muscles and the gas shortage.

"Ouch! That hurt!" Joe complained.

"Sorry. We could go to the American Embassy. They'll help us find gas."

"Sure they will. They'll give us gas to go home."

"We have to go on to the Galapagos," Pat said. "I don't care if we get back home or not, but we have to get there."

"Besides," David agreed, "we've almost made it already."

"Not quite." Joe laughed. "I don't think my shoulder muscles have ever been this sore."

"We don't want to go back," David said. "I can just imagine the 'I told you so' crap we'd get."

"You guys wouldn't get it like I would."

Heather nodded. "Your friends are a nuisance, Gwen. I think all of us agree we should keep going south."

"Are the tanks completely empty?" Pat asked.

"No, there's quite a bit of fuel left in one of them."

"Enough to get us to Teguchigulpa?"

"Now there's a possibility. Let's have a look." David grabbed a map from Joe's bag.

"That's a fine last resort," Heather said. "We should have one more shot at officialdom. There has to be some way to get gas. I want to try those people at the airport again."

"And tell them what?" I asked.

"That we're scientists. Pat and I don't have Ph.D.'s for nothing."

"Perfect," David agreed. "We'll describe our scientific expedition."

"You guys are too much," I said. "We're just a bunch of tourists—"

"How can you say that? We've been studying the flora and fauna of the Galapagos all year. And we'll work hard while we're there. Exactly what constitutes a scientific expedition?"

"I can't say for sure, but I know this isn't one."

"You got a better idea?"

"No, unfortunately."

"O.K. So tomorrow we go on the attack."

Apparently hot showers were available that night. I never figured out how to work the heating device in the shower head.

So I had my traditional cold shower and fell into bed, too tired to notice whether or not it was comfortable.

CHAPTER SIX

Managua, Nicaragua to Rio Hatto, Panama

1. Gasolino

T he breakfast coffee was strong enough to get my attention. I sipped my third cup while the others ate. They had recovered from the frightening experience at the airport and were plotting strategy. I hadn't, and I was worried sick.

"Maybe we should just give up and go back home." I ignored Pat's dirty look.

"Nonsense," David replied. "We'll have our gas and be on our way by noon." He reached for more bacon.

"I just thought of something." Heather set her teacup down loudly. "We should tell them the Ecuadorian military is making arrangements for us."

"You mean the gas they're taking to the islands for our return flight?" Pat asked. "That's hardly making arrangements."

"Heather's right," David said. "That could be important. Do you have the letter?"

"It's here somewhere." She patted her bag.

"Have some more sausage," I suggested. "You need your strength for the negotiations."

It was seven when the taxi arrived. The others bade the hostess a jocular farewell, but even their moods turned sober as we neared the city. The devastation, first viewed in the soft rays of twilight, was starkly revealed by the brilliant early morning sun. David stopped for a picture before a fallen structure. The walls of the house were lying at angry angles like a broken doll house. Anyone at home at the time of the earthquake would be long dead, entombed like Egyptian pharaohs with the paraphernalia of their lives.

We drove in silence and were relieved to reach the relative sanity of the airport.

I volunteered to wait with the luggage. I wanted time to catch up on my notes, but couldn't concentrate. The plastic chair reminded me of our detention, and I squirmed. It was cooler and less humid, but the pervasive moldy smell was nauseating. The flies, buzzing endlessly around me, were driving me crazy. I tried to focus on the environment. The room was dominated by scaffolding. Enormous cracks ran down the walls in a pattern of disaster.

A workman dragged a hose across the waiting room, then abandoned it by my feet—a languishing, red-rubbed black rubber snake. I heard a familiar voice—Carlos—on the other side of the room. He smiled and waved. When I didn't respond, he laughed. Humiliated, I pretended to concentrate on my writing.

And then David came rushing up. He was out of breath. "Get your stuff. We're going back to the city."

"Why on earth?"

"To find the office of the Director of Civil Aviation."

"What's he got to do with us?"

"He's the only one in Nicaragua with the authority to grant us gasolino."

"You go. I'll wait here. I don't want to drive through Managua again."

"It's not a good idea to split up the group," Heather said.

"What have you got against Managua?"

"It's the people—the cold, hungry, desperate people. It's not right for us to move in and out of their tragedy like we're in a movie theater. What we're seeing out there is reality. We can't just go on with our lives as if nothing had happened."

"But what would you have us do?" Heather asked.

"I don't know. But I hate being there."

"It may seem insensitive," Pat said, "But we don't have much choice. We have to get out of here. And we can't afford to get separated. Things are crazy enough."

"I suppose you're right." I picked up my bag and Pat's camera.

"I'll carry it," she said.

"You sure?"

Heather paused at the doorway. "David, how much did you tip our driver?"

"Enough that he'll welcome us back. Come on."

We retraced our torturous route through the city, only to find ourselves in a familiar neighborhood.

"Isn't this the street the pension is on?" Joe asked.

"What an amazing coincidence," Heather said.

"This is really dumb," I commented. "We could have slept until nine and walked here after breakfast."

"If you're so smart, why didn't you suggest that?" David asked.

"Sorry. Didn't mean to complain. But why are we stopping in front of a private home?"

"Because this is the address they gave us. The office must have been moved here after the quake. Most of the government buildings were leveled."

"Let's go find the man." David was already on his feet. "Grab your bags."

"But David, the bags will detract from our image. Proper scientists would have things like that under control, wouldn't they?" Heather asked.

"I'll stay with the bags," I volunteered. "I can't stand the sight of blood. Have you decided what this expedition is studying?"

"The variation in webbing thickness among the masked, red, and blue footed boobies. That means we have to hit a lot of islands."

"Most impressive. Have a good chat." I waved them on and settled into my book.

It wasn't long before David returned and stuck his head in the window. "The Director hasn't arrived."

"Any idea how long he'll be?"

"No. Nobody speaks English. We showed them the notice about no gas and pointed at ourselves. Joe even tried flapping his arms. They just laughed."

"I don't blame them. Are you sure the Director's coming today?"

"No. But at least we're occupying his office. We can stage a sit-in if he doesn't turn up by nightfall."

"I'll look forward to that. Keep up the good work. And you might think about drawing a picture next time. Flapping arms are subject to misinterpretation."

"Good point."

I gave up trying to read and watched the activity in the street. Cars and trucks honked their way through the throngs of people. Many were bent under wares to sell and bundles of firewood. Their skinny bodies told their stories, but it was the eyes that haunted me, the empty eyes of hopelessness, acceptance, martyr-dom. Eyes that had lived a nightmare. Their sorrow touched my soul, but I was an invisible alien, witnessing their drama from behind one-way glass. My eyes were as intrusive as David's camera lens, and yet I couldn't stop watching.

It was a long time before David reappeared, and I was beginning to worry. "The Director arrived," he said, "But he doesn't speak English, either."

"Why don't we hire that German lady at the pension? She could translate for Heather."

"It may come to that," David agreed. "He's moved us out of his office. We'll have to rethink our sit-in."

"What's everybody doing?"

"They're trying to find some useful phrases in Joe's Spanish book."

"I'll bet they can't find 'scientific expedition to the Galapagos'."

"We'd better find it somewhere or we're in the soup. Keep cool."

He had just left, striding purposefully back to the house, when a station wagon pulled up. The driver opened a table next to the taxi and began laying out an assortment of luncheon dishes. Secretaries poured from the building to check the repast, then rushed back inside to get orders. It was one of the few carefree scenes I witnessed in Managua.

When the frenzy ended, I struggled out to buy six bananas. Not exactly lunch, but it would keep us from passing out.

I handed one to the driver as a peace offering. He pointed at his watch.

"I'm sorry about the delay," I said.

He pointed at his watch again. I sympathized, but, not wanting to be left on the curb with our belongings, I shook my head and climbed back in. I wondered what kind of tip David had really given him that morning. I stuck my head in my book and waited. It must have been thirty minutes before they all came running out of the building.

"We have it!" Joe fell into the cab on top of me. "We have authorization to get gas!"

"Airport, please," David said to the driver who was smiling with relief. "They found a guy who speaks idiomatic English."

"Where?"

"Right there, in the office. He's a mechanic, and he trained in California. Now he's Assistant Director of Civil Aviation. He walked in and said, 'I heard about you. The airport people thought you were the notorious weapons smugglers who fly around in a Cherokee. Your registration number is just enough like the culprits' that they were sure you were it'."

"So it was real. We really were in danger."

"According to him, we could have been in a hell of a lot of trouble," Pat said. "We asked him a lot of questions, and then he wanted to hear our side of it. He was sympathetic, but he said we should have written for permission to land."

"We did write," Heather said. "David and I spent hours on those letters."

"We sent them to every possible landing place in Central and South America," David added. "But they couldn't find it. We should have brought a copy with us."

"So why did he give us the gas?" I asked.

"Because he believed us," Pat said. "He thinks we're a bunch of nuts to do this, but he believes our story. Everybody else thought it was some kind of cover. We were really lucky. This guy knows enough Americans to tell the difference."

"While the letter was being typed, he talked a blue streak. I thought he'd never stop. We had to hear all about the earthquake, rebuilding plans for the city, his experiences in California—"

"Don't forget the expeditions into the mountains of Nicaragua—"

"Did you tell him about the boobies?" I asked.

"No need. We'll save it for next time."

"God preserve us. Here, have a banana."

2. Panic over Panama

Joe taxied to the end of the field and pulled up at the gas pump. The inside of the plane was like a sauna, and we were delighted to escape for a moment. The dispensers of gas spoke English, and I chatted with them as we drank Cokes in the small diner.

"The Galapagos, you say. Are you a missionary?"

I shook my head in amazement. From whore to missionary in less than twenty-four hours. My self image would never be the same.

"Hey, Gwen, you coming with us?"

"Just thought I'd let you do the waiting for once." I climbed aboard and checked my flight gear: books, paper, pencils: the essentials.

"Can we fly over the city?" Heather asked.

"No. Overflights are forbidden."

"Why in hell—" David said. "We should had the director write a letter for us."

"We are not going back to Managua," Pat said.

"No?" Joe laughed. "How about you, Gwen? Want to go back to the city?"

"You've got to be kidding." I was secretly relieved that our flyover request had been denied. The pattern of devastation as seen from a taxi was puzzling, but curiosity could not be a sufficient excuse for such an arrogant act.

Joe closed his door, and moments later I noticed the pungent smell of gasoline. "Joe, I smell gas."

"56 Whiskey calling the tower. Over."

"Joe, hello up there. I smell gas."

"We just filled up, remember? They always spill some of it."

"I've never smelled it like this before—"

"Hey, kid, you worry too much. It'll blow away as soon as we're airborne."

"Why do I have the feeling you're ignoring me?"

He ignored the question, listening instead to the instructions from the tower. And my anxiety melted when we lifted off.

Joe circled into our course, and we had a final glimpse of Managua. And then it was gone. We had escaped. The agony of the city had already become remembered pain.

I poked Joe in the back. "How far is it to Panama City?"

"We'll land at Tocuman International before nightfall. I promise."

"In time for a good dinner?" I asked.

"Right. My treat. There's a storm on the coast, so we're going out of our way. The good news is, we'll be flying over Lake Nicaragua."

Lake Managua is lovely, but Lake Nicaragua is indescribably lovelier. Set in emerald hillsides rising to magnificent gray volcanos, its waters are a prism reflecting all the colors of the spectrum.

As the motor droned on, I tried to watch the changing landscape below. It was dazzling, compelling, yet I was finding it increasingly hard to concentrate. Perhaps the iridescent water was hypnotic. I was unaccountably sleepy, and soon drifted into a pleasant doze.

When I awakened, someone told me we were over Puentarenas, Costa Rica. There was still a faint smell of gas in the air, constantly recirculating past our noses. I noted in my journal that it was more intense at the start of inhalation. We were tantalizingly close to the last clouds of the rainy season. Joe had heard there was flooding in San Jose.

The storm was moving north, towing plump clouds that scuttled along on sanded bottoms. A migration of smaller clouds, suspended in a vaporous cocoon, moved past the window. The bay to the left was enclosed by green, sunlit hills held firmly in place by the storm. To the right, misty islands were carefully seated in a gray, shimmering ocean. Above, the radiant sky was sliced open by a single, long cirrus cloud, thin from hurrying after the storm.

I turned to speak to Pat and Heather, but they were fast asleep. So I shared rice crackers and dried apples with Joe and David. The taste of gasoline lingered despite a cupful of drinking-fountain water.

A storm cloud approached—or were we approaching it? It looked hungry, its mouth gaping open before us. Yet, when we broke into its skinless being, it only tossed us about a bit as it laughed at our armature and the tickles of our wingtips.

And then we were above the storm. Thunderheads rose to the left. A sea of inky blackness stretched below in all directions. The gas fumes were still strong. It was four-fifteen by somebody's time, and we were somewhere over Panama. I wondered if it was Tuesday and was glad I wasn't sure.

"Joe, I still smell gas."

"It must be on your clothes. We aren't getting it up here."

"You wouldn't notice if you did." My head ached and I didn't want to move. But it seemed important to check on Pat and Heather. I struggled around in my seat. Pat's face was gray and she was breathing with difficulty. "Are you all right?" She didn't respond. "Heather," I shouted, "Pat needs oxygen. Help me wake her." Heather's eyes were wide open, fixed on me, but she didn't answer. I turned around and poked Joe in the back. "I can't get Heather and Pat to talk to me."

"Finally wore them out, did you?" Joe laughed.

"Damn it, this is important. Pat should be on oxygen."

"We're not that high. She's O.K. Stop worrying. David, open that map for me."

I slumped down in my seat and tried to think. I had to do something, but what? Maybe if I wrote it down— I stared blankly at the notepad in my lap. It was so hard to move. My body felt separate—as if it were floating a few feet away. If I shut my eyes for a minute, I'd remember—

I was jolted back into reality by a deafening silence. The engine had stopped. At first I thought it was the momentary lull associated with switching gas tanks. But the silence was interrupted only by the grinding of the starter. My adrenaline surged as I listened to Joe and David's startlingly clear voices:

"They're really empty," Joe said.

"Impossible," David replied. "We had enough gas to make Colombia."

"That may be, but, except for a small amount in number two, the tanks are empty."

"Can we make Tocuman?"

"No way." Joe shook his head. "We have fifteen minutes, max." He restarted the engine, then called Tocuman. "We're out of gas," he told the controller.

"56 Whiskey, are you sure?"

"Affirmative. We're turning toward the coast to find a landing spot. 56 Whiskey over and out." Joe looked back at me. "An emergency landing will be easier along the ocean."

"Is this really happening?"

" 'Fraid so. Sorry."

In the next few minutes we might crash. In the next few minutes we might die. I looked down at the rock studded hillside below. I knew I should be terrified, but I wasn't. I'd long since come to terms with the possibility of disaster. And if I had to die relatively young, this was one hell of a way to do it. I felt intensely alive, and whatever happened now, the experience was mine.

I turned to check on my buddies. Pat was still out of it, but Heather was wide awake. "I guess this is it," I said. "Will you join me in a last supper?"

"What a good idea." She smiled uneasily.

I poured water into two cups and she found the dried apples. We dined in silence, then solemnly shook hands. There was nothing more to say.

I turned back to stare out the window. We were flying toward enormous black clouds that dwarfed our plane. Joe veered sharply away from them. Beneath us, vivid, green, rolling hills were shadowed by the storm. The scene was pastoral, more like Wisconsin than the tropics, and decidedly inappropriate for a landing. Where would we be in an hour? On the ground, for sure. The question was, where and how.

3. Rio Hatto

Joe's shout was jubilant. "Look! A landing strip!"

"A paved landing strip," David added. "Must be for jets."

"In the middle of nowhere?" I asked.

"Don't get picky. It's here, and we're going in."

Joe tried to radio the tower plainly visible below, but couldn't rouse them. Finally, he called Tocuman.

"That's Rio Hatto," the controller said. "Are you sure you're out of gas? It would be better not to land at Rio Hatto."

"There is no way, I repeat, no way we can make Tocuman. Wherever we are, we're going in."

The controller agreed to alert Rio Hatto and Joe turned his attention to landing. Surprisingly, it was the smoothest arrival of the trip—like alighting on glass.

As we taxied back toward the tower, a young man in a yellow shirt came trotting down the runway. Motioning with the butt of his rifle, he directed us to a parking spot. Joe had just turned off the engine when the Tocuman controller came on the air to ask if we were all right.

"56 Whiskey down safely. Thank you. Over and out."

"We made it! We're down!" I shrieked.

Heather smiled, and Pat, who was wide awake, nodded.

"How do you feel?" I asked.

"I'm fine. But what's all this water doing on the floor? My shoes are soaked."

I put my hand into the puddle. It felt cold. I smelled my fingers. "That's not water. It's gasoline. My God! Joe, there's an inch of gas on the floor of the cabin."

"Gas? You mean—"

"Let me see that—" David stretched over the back of his seat to touch the floor by my feet. "She's right. There's a leak in the fuel system."

"Jesus Christ!" Joe yelled. "We could have blown up. One spark—"

"We've got to find that leak," David interrupted. "Everyone out of here, now!"

"How could there be a leak in the cabin—" I asked.

"You know damn well how," David snapped. "My God damned fuel line modifications."

Hurriedly we collected our gear from the floor and the top of the life raft. Our joy over the successful landing had flattened into shock. I hardly noticed when Yellow Shirt, accompanied by another rifle-bearing youth, tapped on the outside of the cabin.

"Buenas días," he shouted.

Heather opened the side door. "¿Habla inglés?" But of course he didn't.

Joe climbed onto the wing. "No gasolino."

Yellow Shirt nodded and gestured toward the fuel tank. Laughing, he called to his friend who ran off. We stumbled out into the fresh clean air and tested our shaky legs.

Suddenly we heard a dreadful clatter in the distance. It was several minutes before an ancient station wagon, vintage 1930, chugged into view. Yellow Shirt beamed as his friend brought the rusty heap to a halt in front of us. He gestured to Joe to get in.

"What's going on?" Heather asked.

"Looks like they're taking us to get gas," I said. "See you guys later."

I grabbed my purse and started toward the car, but Yellow Shirt politely pushed me aside. "Il piloto."

"Joe, I don't think you should go alone—"

He shrugged and jumped in with Yellow Shirt. The car made strange screeching noises, backfired, and began to move. It listed to the left, and the left rear wheel wobbled ominously. Every few feet it paused, bucked, and backfired again. Still dazed, we stood in silence, watching it slowly disappear.

It was Pat who broke the silence. "Heather, where is Joe's passport?"

"In my purse." Heather wet her lips. "That's not too good, is it?"

"Look at it this way," Pat replied. "When he gets mugged, he won't lose it."

"How comforting."

"Damn!" David was shouting behind us. "Come here and help me with this Godawful mess." He was leaning into the plane, wrench in hand. "I have to take this seat out to get at the fuel line connections, and your stuff is in the way."

"Everything has to come out." Heather peered under David's arm. "It all reeks of gasoline. Here, Gwen, put these somewhere." She handed me the two wet jackets she had retrieved from the cabin floor.

"Would you mind if I made a quick pit stop first?"

"This'll just take a minute. David's in a real snit."

"Why am I the only one in this group with normal human needs?" No one answered. I tried unsuccessfully to wring out the jackets before hanging them over a nearby branch. Gasoline was dripping from the sleeves, and I was grateful for the slight breeze and near ninety degree temperature.

We worked in silence, and in half an hour had most of our belongings spread across the landscape—from the doors and tail of the plane to the grass, rocks, and trees. I was just about to take my long-overdue pit stop when a jeep pulled up beside the plane. A wiry young soldier jumped out and looked nervously around. Gradually, a second, heavy-set man emerged from the far side. Both were carrying rifles.

"Hello," I said. "¿Habla inglés?"

"No. ¿Habla español?"

"We ran out of gas," I volunteered.

"Gasolino," David said. "Il piloto went—" He pointed as if at the retreating car.

The soldiers laughed and asked something is Spanish.

"Gasolino," David replied loudly. "No español."

"That won't help, David," Heather said. "They can't understand a word you're saying."

"How do you know that?"

The soldiers were talking again, and I could make out only occasional words:

"…CIA…FBI…"

"No," I shouted. "We're scientists—"

"When did you convert?" David asked.

I ignored him. "Scientific expedition."

"FBI," they replied.

"David, he just called you 'Sergeant.' He thinks we have military connections."

"Could be worse," David said.

Pat gave up, but the rest of us continued to try even though communication was impossible. Each time one of us spoke, the younger man would burst into laughter, then shout a question in Spanish. Our English answer, complete with gestures, would send him into gales of laughter and, before long, all of us would join in.

The fat soldier drove off—we assumed to get reinforcements—but our jumpy friend stayed with us, watching our every move. We were nervous, ourselves. It seemed an eternity before David managed to unfasten the seat. It was hard to appear nonchalant while taking the airplane apart. And reality was sinking in. The smell of gas almost made me gag. Boots that had been stowed on the cabin floor were soaked through, towels reeked. How could we have ignored this lethal situation for so long?

Finally we pulled the seat out of the plane and onto the grass. I glanced at the guard. He had rounded the tail and was leaning casually on the wing. Joe would have been furious—except when boarding the plane, he didn't allow us to so much as touch the wings. But I wasn't about to tell the guard to move. He was watching us, but he didn't seem at all curious about what we were doing. Apparently his assignment was to keep us corralled, and, if we spent our time rebuilding the airplane, that was fine with him.

"Do you think he'll let me go bushing?" I asked Heather.

"Why wouldn't he?"

I pointed to myself, then the bushes, smiled, and started off. The guard pointed his rifle at me and motioned me back toward the plane. He smiled pleasantly.

"He may live to regret that," I said.

"So may we all," Pat agreed.

I was horrified to see that a gas-soaked towel was hanging on the cabin door, inches from the guard's face. If he went into a swoon, we'd be arrested for attacking him. But the breeze must have been in the other direction, because he didn't react. I was just beginning to relax when he pulled out a pack of cigarettes and indicated that he needed a match.

"No!" I screamed, gesturing wildly. The others froze, watching him as he shrugged and pocketed the cigarettes. I kept a close eye on the guard while David poked around in the cabin. It wasn't clear what he was doing in there, and his exclamations didn't help: "Jesus H. Christ! …Unbelievable!…My God, I really goofed…"

"Hurry up, David," I whispered. "They'll never let us out of here if they see what you've done to the fuel lines."

"Stop being paranoid," he said. "They don't give one hot damn what we do."

"You don't know that—"

"Where's that Goddamned screwdriver?"

I moved out of Heather's way. David worked for a few more minutes and then emerged to give us the diagnosis. It was simple enough. His design of the fuel line modifications was fine, but he had failed to tighten the connections after everything was in place, and the vibrations had loosened them to the leaking point.

David was shaken by the magnitude of his mistake, and I knew he would tighten things carefully this time. What worried me was that he might have made other modifications we didn't know about. If we cross-examined him, he'd think we'd lost faith in his judgment. If we didn't—

It was an impossible dilemma. I put it out of my mind. There was plenty of work to be done and more than enough to think about. David was ordering us about like handmaidens, and everything in the plane needed to be wiped down and aired. I was hanging towels on a tree limb when Pat beckoned me to the far side of the plane.

"I'm worried about Joe," she whispered.

"I'm worried about us. We're being held captive by soldiers who have no idea why we're here or what we might do, and we can't communicate with them."

"But don't you see? Joe is missing, and we can't even ask them to look for him. We assumed that Yellow Shirt was part of the military here, but everyone else we've seen is in uniform—"

"But Yellow Shirt seemed so friendly—"

"Gwen, hand me that wrench," David yelled, and I sprang into action. At least this was something I could do.

4. Finding an interpreter

David worked furiously, focusing his considerable intensity on completing the job. Even so, it was dusk when we started putting the innards of the plane back in place. The middle seat was the hardest part. Once that was reinstalled, it was a matter of repacking the survival stuff and all of our possessions.

We had just finished when the base commander arrived, accompanied by our fat friend and several subordinates.

"My God!" I said. "Look at that station wagon. There are bars on the back window. They've come to arrest us."

"Nonsense," David replied. "They're just coming for a visit. Let me talk to him."

I was offended by his assumption that he could cope with any situation. "But you don't speak Spanish," I said.

"A mere detail, girl. Stand aside."

Quaking in my dank sneakers, I followed the others to the station wagon and was surprised to find the commander in a pleasant mood. Patiently he asked several questions in Spanish, and we shouted answers in English. Both groups reacted to this impasse with raised voices and frantic arm movements, as if emphasis could bridge the language barrier. Finally the commander held up his hand in a mute request for silence. We all shut up.

"Il piloto intérprete," he announced.

The soldiers standing around him nodded and smiled admiringly.

"What's he saying?" I asked David.

"I think he's talking about an English speaking pilot," David replied.

Everyone nodded and laughed some more, and then the commander and most of his staff drove off, leaving only two soldiers to keep watch over us.

"So," I said, "This is definitely a turn for the better."

"I wish Joe would turn up," David said.

"He should be back by now," Heather said. "I wonder if he ran out of money."

"He had plenty of cash," David replied. "No, I'd be willing to bet they got lost."

"But he doesn't have his passport," I reminded him. "And he didn't immigrate properly. Don't they arrest people for that?"

"You're right, Gwen," Heather said. "He's probably in jail."

Pat, who was sitting all hunched up on a fallen log, said, "More likely he's been hit over the head, robbed, and left for dead in a ditch."

"Pat, that doesn't sound like you." I said.

"I don't feel much like me. We should never have let him go alone."

"We should do something—" I said.

"Like what?" David asked. "We have no idea where he is, and we can't talk to anybody."

We were still arguing when Heather said, "Here comes the Commandante. Perhaps he brought help."

A handsome young lieutenant stepped out of the station wagon and walked toward us, hand extended. "Hello there. What brings you to Rio Hatto?" he said, in flawless English.

5. Aviation fuel

Piloto-intérprete Moreno was amused when we all talked at once, and somehow he managed to sort out our story. A jet pilot who had spent two years training at Lackland Air Force Base in San Antonio, Texas, he interceded for us and, thanks to him, the Commandante decided we were not spies. This settled, the Commandante told his staff to fix up the guest trailer so that we could get a good night's sleep. Then he had our stuff bags packed into the station wagon and delivered to the trailer door.

We were telling Lieutenant Moreno about our missing pilot when an ancient station wagon pulled up. Joe, Yellow Shirt, and friend, jumped out looking frightfully pleased with themselves.

"I take it that smile means you bought gas?"

"Right again, Gwen. It was a great adventure."

"You were gone five hours. It's almost dark. Did they take you to Acapulco?"

"That car doesn't go over ten miles an hour. And the town is small. We had trouble finding aviation fuel."

"Where did you buy it?"

"At a corner gas station." He laughed.

"Be serious."

"I am serious. That's where we bought it."

"How do you know it's aviation fuel?"

"It's green. It smells like gas. What more do you want?"

"I want to know if we can take off in the morning."

"You worry too much. Come on. We've got to get this stuff into the plane."

Working by flashlight, Joe, David and Yellow Shirt filtered the newly purchased gas through a chamois and into the fuel tanks. I gave up and walked to the trailer. Pat and Heather had already started organizing our belongings.

"You O.K.?" I asked Pat.

"Just a little tired," she replied. "Tired and hungry."

"There must be food somewhere. Come on, Heather, let's find dinner."

We dove into the camping supplies looking for anything edible. We weren't feeling fussy. It was nine, and it had been a long time since our twelve-thirty bananas in Managua. Heather found a can opener and we opened three cans of beans, heated coffee water, and collapsed exhausted onto the ancient furniture. When Joe and David came in, we ate in silence.

We had just finished and were lapsing into a pleasant torpor when we heard a knock at the door. We tried to ignore it, but it recurred, louder. I staggered up and opened the door for Lieutenant Moreno.

"How nice of you to drop by," I said. "We're very grateful for your help. Would you like some hot chocolate?"

"Thanks," he replied. "I'd love it. I was glad to help. The people in San Antonio were great to me. You know, I've only been back here one week."

"You mean if we'd come two weeks ago, there wouldn't have been anyone to interpret for us?"

"Right. Good timing, wasn't it? I had a wonderful time in Texas. Last year I broke my leg playing softball, but an American Major took care of me. He pushed me around in a wheelchair. What a great guy!"

Our cumulative exhaustion was taking its toll, and it was hard to concentrate on the lieutenant's stories. He was telling us about the arrogant American civilians living in Panama. He said

Panamanians liked American tourists and American military, but hated the residents.

He teased Pat about being so quiet, unaware that she was, in fact, asleep. The wonder of it was that any of us were able to respond. It was almost eleven when he noticed we were all nodding off and stood up to leave. He paused at the door.

"Where do you go from here?"

"Buenaventura, Colombia," Joe said. "Then on to Guayaquil, Ecuador."

"That's crazy. I'd never make a flight like that. Do you realize, if your plane goes down, the jungle will cover it over in just a few hours? You'll simply disappear. Besides, there is no search and rescue operation in South America. No one will miss you if you're overdue."

On that reassuring note, he took his leave. It was some indication of our general state of fatigue that we hardly noticed his comments.

CHAPTER SEVEN
Rio Hatto, Panama to Guayaquil, Ecuador

1. Regrouping

had a restless night. The chorus of rusty bedsprings suggested the others were equally uncomfortable. I had just fallen into a deep sleep when Heather's alarm sounded. My watch said five-fifteen. I staggered into the kitchen and turned on the water.

A glance out the dirty window revealed the idyllic landscape we had missed in the dark. Early-morning meadow-green sharpened as sunlight pushed reluctant shadows under rolling hills. I could hear troops drilling. They sounded close, but I couldn't see them through the forest of ancient trees. The longer I listened, the more incongruous it seemed—marching feet, voices shouting cadence, the whole military presence in this paradise.

"Is there coffee?" David was leaning against the door jamb. He looked terrible. Remorse had aged him.

"The water's heating. Why are we up so early?"

"We have to make Guayaquil by nightfall."

"Guayaquil, Ecuador? Are you crazy?"

"We have to be in the Galapagos tomorrow. That's when the Bronzewing charter begins. Heather arranged for us to be picked up at noon at the Baltra airstrip."

"That's out of the question. We must get some rest."

"Sorry," David replied. "We don't have time to rest."

"Be reasonable. We can call the Bronzewing agent in Guayaquil and tell him we've been delayed. This is only Wednesday. We can still make connections with the charter flight on Friday."

"We're not taking the charter flight." I hadn't seen Heather come in. "We made that decision months ago. David, did you find your socks?"

"Yes."

"We made that decision before the emergency landing," I corrected. "That changes everything."

David picked up the instant coffee and unscrewed the lid. "Gwen's nervous because I messed up."

"I'm nervous because you're all being too casual. You were from the start, but I couldn't prove it until something went wrong."

"Jesus H. Christ!" David exploded. "I fixed the God damned leak. It won't happen again."

"Maybe not, but chances are something else will. Listen, David, Moreno says it's risky to fly over the jungle. For God's sake, anyone with an ounce of common sense would agree we should start out rested."

"I told you. There isn't time to rest. The Bronzewing is waiting."

"I'm talking about one day to check the plane."

"So that's it. You want to hire a mechanic to go over my fixes."

"Fixes? Is that a plural? What besides the fuel line did you fix?"

"Nothing!"

"I think we've discussed this long enough, don't you?" Heather asked. "Who wants eggs?"

"I'm out of the bathroom." Joe was pale from lack of sleep.

"It's about time." David stomped out.

"Joe, don't you think we need a day off?" I asked. "Pat's tired. She can't take much more of this kind of pressure—"

"I'm fine." Pat struggled out of the cocoon she had fashioned on the couch.

"You don't look fine. Pat, these people are talking about flying all the way to Guayaquil today."

"Of course. We don't want to miss the Bronzewing."

I did a slow burn while the others ate. There was no point in arguing. They were all nuts. We rushed through our cereal and gulped boiled coffee out of tin cups.

"Damn it, the cup burned my lips," I said.

"You should have let it cool," David replied. "Where's your common sense?"

"That's a damned good question," I snapped. No one responded, and I jumped up to wash the dishes. The others rolled sleeping bags, stepped on each other, argued over bathroom access, and repacked. By six, we were lugging our belongings back to the plane.

"We're doing this ass backwards," I said to Joe. "We don't have the papers from the Commandante, and we can't go anywhere without them."

"Lieutenant Moreno said the guard would have the papers for us this morning. What difference does it make?"

"The instant coffee's packed, that's the difference. I'll bet our own private guard does not have the papers, and I won't be able to get another cup of coffee until Panama International."

"God, lady, how you worry. You'll have your coffee by nine-thirty. The guard probably has our papers in his pocket. When we're ready to go, he'll give them to us."

"He doesn't and he won't."

"Trust me," Joe said.

I wasn't convinced, but there wasn't any point in arguing. Joe unlocked the plane and we packed our sleeping bags back into the forward hatch and secured it carefully. When all our gear was loaded, I said, "Now are you ready to talk to the guard?"

"Might as well," Joe replied. "Where is he?"

"He went thataway." I pointed toward the woods.

"Thanks for nothing."

David and Joe went after the guard, and soon returned with him in tow.

"We found him, but he doesn't have the faintest idea what we want." David was standing in front of us, hands on his hips, jaw tightly clenched under my straw hat.

"What a surprise," I said sarcastically.

"Let's go find the Commandante," David said. "Or Lieutenant Moreno."

"Moreno told us they'd both be gone this morning," Pat said.

"I thought you slept through all that."

"Not the good part."

"Well, then, we'll have to find someone else," David replied.

"Maybe no one else is authorized to let us go," Pat suggested.

"Now you're worrying. It's contagious. Try to relax."

"Relax?" Heather joined in. "Those male chauvinists officers won't even allow women in the room with them. I feel powerless."

"Why am I enjoying this?" David smirked.

"Watch it, David," I said.

"We will return with papers. Don't leave without us."

Joe, David and the trusty guard walked down the road toward headquarters.

"Nothing like the good old hurry up and wait routine," Heather said. "I think I'll lie down in the meadow and sleep."

She stretched out in the shade of a nearby tree.

I glared at Pat. "Thanks for your generous support."

"What's that about?"

"It's about getting some much needed rest tonight."

"We don't have time."

"We had time for the gas leak," I said. "You want to see it happen again?"

"It won't. David fixed it. What concerns me is that he may have done something else to the plane."

"Yeah. Heather must know what he did. Maybe we should talk to her."

"Are you crazy? She's much too busy playing house with David to pay attention to his fuel line modifications."

"He's attractive," I said. "I can understand that. What I don't understand is you. You're ill. You need rest."

"There's nothing wrong with me. I've waited all my life for this trip. I'm not going to risk missing the Bronzewing."

"How the hell did I get mixed up with this bunch of idiots? A middle-aged scientist reliving her youth, a pilot playing with his new instruments, a twenty-five-year-old madman who thinks the plane is his own tinker-toy set, and you. You'd rather die than miss one day in the Galapagos. You've all got your own private agendas, don't you?"

"That beats not bothering to have one. If you dislike our agendas so much, why don't you catch the next flight out of Tocuman."

"I might just do that." I found a pleasant spot under a tree and tried to imagine how it would be to go home, to see the animals, my friends— A familiar feeling of dreariness stirred. I would have to face my work, my music, my self. The excitement of the last few days had driven away depression. I was feeling more alive than I had in a year. Maybe surrounding myself with lunatics wasn't such a bad idea.

The chapel bell was ringing, signaling what? Mass or mess? I settled back against a tree trunk. The grass smelled sweet. A dozen bird songs intertwined above me. This was a magical, pastoral wonderland, in no particular place. I looked at the plane. It seemed relaxed, too, as if waiting suited it. Pat's straw hat, hanging by the open door, was swinging slowly back and forth in the breeze. I didn't want to go home.

2. Aviation Fuel

David and Joe made several trips to headquarters, accompanied by our guard and Yellow Shirt. It was after seven when they returned with the papers. In all, the delay had cost us little more than an hour. By our standards, that hardly counted.

As we boarded the plane, I realized I was terrified. "Joe, do something. I'm scared."

"About what?"

"The gas. You aren't even sure it's aviation fuel."

"I've got it all figured out. I'll take off using the last of the Managua gas. We didn't add anything to that tank last night. Once we're airborne, the other fuel would get us to Tocuman even if it was low octane."

"Are you sure of that?"

"Pretty sure. But to be on the safe side, I'm going to check it out while we're still in easy range of Rio Hatto."

"What do you mean, 'check it out?'"

"I'll stop the engine and try to restart using one of the tanks that has new gas in it."

"Not that again."

"Is everyone set? We should get started."

We closed the doors, waved farewell to Yellow Shirt, and made a routine takeoff.

As we came out of the climb, Joe shouted, "I'm ready for the test."

I looked back at Heather. She was chalk white, but still able to smile. Pat appeared unperturbed. I couldn't tell anything from the back of David's head.

Then the engine stopped. There was a grim, seemingly endless, period of silence while Joe switched tanks and tried the ignition. And, miraculously, the engine turned over comfortably and resumed its cacophonous roar. Evidently, it was quite content to consume Panamanian gas of whatever octane. Our excited exclamations were drowned out by the noise, but looks and gestures indicated that Joe was enormously pleased with himself. I was weak with relief.

It was a beautiful flight. The coastline was studded with a series of small, intensely green, rock-crested islands. I was enjoying the early morning ocean, crinkled like aluminum foil stretched over an enormous undulating python, when Heather poked me in the back.

"Do you think Joe will be in trouble for landing at a military base?"

"Lieutenant Moreno said the papers would take care of everything."

"I hope you're right."

"You're reading my script. I'm the designated worrier."

"The military's out of my line. If they detain him, our schedule's shot to hell."

"Did you mention in your correspondence that we might be late arriving in the Galapagos?" I shouted.

"It never occurred to me."

"Of course not. I wonder what we'll find to do on Baltra for three weeks."

"There it is," David shouted. "The Panama Canal."

The ocean was sprinkled with ships all pointing toward the canal entrance as if being sucked into an invisible funnel. Under the arch, a sedate, single file proceeded toward the first lock.

"Ask Joe if we can fly over," Heather said. "I want to see one of the locks."

"Joe, can we fly over?" I shouted.

"No. It's illegal, and I don't need any more black marks on my record."

"Damn!" Heather said. "Joe's turning into a real spoil sport."

"Isn't he, though?"

3. Panama International

We landed at the large, international airport a little after eight and were surprised when Joe was directed to park between a 747 and a DC-8. We felt like Lilliputians, crawling out of our tiny plane under the wings of those monsters.

When the gas truck pulled up, I thought we were in great shape. But Joe and David didn't seem to be able to communicate with the driver. Joe took out his wallet and the driver shook his head and gestured as he jabbered away in Spanish. We were mystified. David walked over to us.

"He's made it pretty clear. The only way we can pay for gas is with an international gasoline credit card."

"But we have cash—"

"He won't take cash. International credit card, period."

"What an odd notion," Heather said thoughtfully. "Let me have a try."

She started toward him, but he jumped into the cab and drove away.

"Come on," David said. "Let's go find the authorities. Maybe we can rent a credit card."

"I just hope they don't make a fuss when I present the papers. I'd hate to lose my license." Joe turned to Pat who was sitting in the shade of the wing. "We're heading into the terminal. Are you coming?"

"No, thanks. I'll stay here and read."

"Are you O.K.?" I asked.

"I'm just a little tired."

"It's nine now," Joe said. "We'll be back in thirty minutes."

"I'll expect you at noon."

Heather and I took turns guarding the gear while Joe and David dealt with officialdom. It was only ten when they returned. Joe was jubilant. "I'm off the hook. They didn't give a damn about the leak."

"And look at this," David said. "We have a flight plan AND written permission to pay cash for the gas."

"I'd ask how you did it, but—"

"You don't want to know." Joe steered me toward the door.

We arrived at the plane in high spirits, and were surprised to find Pat in a bad mood.

"I've been harassed," she told us.

"By whom?" Heather asked.

"An airline pilot."

"That sounds like a mild exaggeration."

"It's true. I was sitting here reading when this hot shot in a fancy uniform comes out of the 747. He sees me, and breaks into hysterical laughter. Then he rushes back to the plane, comes out with his camera, and proceeds to take pictures of me and the plane from different angles."

"You must admit the Cherokee looks remarkably out of place between these two whales," I said. "And you're not exactly dressed like a member of the crew."

"I know. But he never acknowledged my presence. I was part of his scene—or maybe subhuman. Anyway, I didn't enjoy being a photo opportunity."

David threw his knapsack on the ground. "Where the bloody hell's the gas truck? They said they'd be right over."

It was an hour before the truck showed up, and Pat had decided she needed to find a restroom.

"Are you too tired to walk to the terminal?" I asked.

"I'd rather not."

"I'll ask the driver if there's one close."

The driver listened sympathetically to my halting request for the ladies' and motioned us into the truck. When he had finished pumping gas, he drove us to the men's locker room at the end of the field and gestured to us to stay put. We heard him shouting at the men inside. I suppose he must have told them to put on their clothes. Then he appeared on the porch and gave us an elaborate "all-clear" signal. As we made our way through the crowd toward the cubicles at the far end of the dressing area, the fully clothed men made loud comments and laughed. They had a wonderful time, and I was delighted not to understand a word they said.

4. Buenaventura, Colombia

I passed around water and raisins when we crossed the Colombian border.

"Here's to South America," Joe said, "and a great Ecuadorian adventure."

"Why don't I hear the tower anymore?" I asked.

"We're out of radio communication."

Lieutenant Moreno had warned us. We had entered a remote wilderness area. There were clouds all around. Joe was following the outskirts of the storm, moving above it, then to its western edge.

"Look at that mountain," David said. "It's not shown on the map."

"Most of South America is unmapped," Joe volunteered. It was information we all could have done without.

He turned inland and the view below changed to a tangled, green landscape. Fragments of muddy, silvery rivers were visible curving gracefully through the dense tropical jungle. Lieutenant Moreno had told us about a group of important officials who had been lost in this area seven years before. Their plane had crashed, and the jungle had devoured it. The air force had searched for weeks but never found a trace of the wreckage. Looking down, I could well imagine it happening. That jungle could consume a battleship in minutes, let alone a small plane. But then, the odds were against having two emergency landings in one trip, weren't they?

It was after one when we reached Buenaventura. The city is a port and appears from the air to be prosperous. Not so the airport. For starters, it's a long way from the city, and we had great difficulty spotting it. Worse, it was ten minutes before we were sure this was, indeed, an airport and not a jungle clearing.

Joe tried several times to contact the tower. "56 Whiskey requesting permission to land. Great, just great. They won't talk to me, and I can't see a wind sock anywhere. Am I blind? Do you see one, Gwen?"

"No. Are you sure we're in the right place?"

"Yes, unfortunately, and I can't circle all day. We'll just have to take a chance. I think the wind's out of the east, right, David?"

"Yes. Look at those trees sway."

It wasn't bad for a guess—off by a mere 180 degrees. The short, rock-paved strip would have been a challenge under the best of circumstances. A tail wind and the added excitement of finding clusters of local residents standing on the runway, made it tough for Joe. The people moved before we hit them, but he was uncomfortable about passing so close to pedestrians.

"Hey, there's the wind sock," David said. "And the wind's coming out of the west."

"I figured that out by myself," Joe replied.

"Gasolino" was a magic word. Two bare-chested members of the airport staff responded immediately by rolling out a barrel and an inner tube. They balanced the barrel on the tube and poured gas into a small bucket. They then filtered the gas from the bucket through a chamois and into the tank.

"Isn't that amazing," I said to Heather. "We're getting faster service here than at Tocuman International."

"You're right. I think I'll take a commemorative photo."

But the staff gestured angrily when she brought out her camera.

"What's wrong?" she asked.

"They don't want to be part of the local scene," Pat replied. "Believe me, it's not fun."

"I wasn't putting them down. Their system is marvelously efficient."

"Maybe they're camera shy," I suggested. "Let's go have a look around."

The airport was in a heavily populated area. Women and children in colorful garb were washing clothes, cutting sugar cane, making their way to and from the river. The landing strip was Main Street. They carried machetes, stalks of sugar cane, and baskets overflowing with laundry, all delicately balanced on their heads.

We returned to the terminal in time to witness a flurry of activity when a DC-3 arrived. After our landing, it was a thrill to see a plane that size stop on such a short runway. Joe was impressed by the pilot's skill, not to mention his uncanny ability to spot the wind sock. Taxis appeared from nowhere to take the travelers to the city and, for a brief moment, the field became a busy airport. But the plane and the taxis left, and within ten minutes the peaceful scene was reestablished.

5. We arrive in Ecuador

We found a refreshment stand and, soft drinks in hand, wearily reboarded the plane. Joe headed back to the ocean. It looked misty out to sea.

We rounded the elbow of South America and met a ferocious branch of the storm. At 6,200 feet, we were above it and did not feel any violence. The farther south we traveled, the more solid the layers of cloud became. They blanketed the ocean as far as the eye could see.

Joe poked my arm. "We're crossing the equator."

"Damn those clouds. I did want to see the red stripe."

"There's the pyramid mountain, Chimhorazo. She's 20,000 feet."

The stunning, snow-white giant, loomed over the clouds, dwarfing the nearby mountain peaks.

"The other peaks are 14,000 feet. That's the range that keeps the cloud bank from drifting inland."

"How far do the clouds extend? Clear out to the Galapagos?"

He nodded. "This is a gigantic storm front."

"Then we'll have to take the charter flight. We'd never spot the islands through these clouds."

"Not to worry. Tomorrow they'll be gone."

"Promise?"

"Promise." He laughed.

"I'm serious."

"I know. I won't take off if there's a cloud in the sky." His eyes twinkled. I didn't believe him for a moment.

I sat back and looked out at white vaporous fluff. The massive, uninterrupted sweep looked powerful, yet safe. I dozed off and dreamed that we had landed smoothly on the clouds.

CHAPTER EIGHT
Guayaquil, Ecuador

1. First glimpse of the city

" Ten minutes to Guayaquil," Joe shouted.

I looked down at the inscrutable cloud bank. "For all I know, we could be landing in France."

He laughed and shook his head. "Woman of little faith."

"What did he say?" Heather yelled in my ear.

"We'll be landing in ten minutes."

"It's about time."

I nodded, but I wasn't thrilled. I had settled into a pleasant torpor and moving would be difficult.

"Here we go!" Joe started the descent, and soon we were immersed in the clouds, plunging through a vast realm of gray, wet nothing. Then, as suddenly as it had appeared, nothingness vanished and we caught our first glimpse of the colorful Ecuadorian landscape. Variegated green hills, pockmarked with glowing, smoky fires, flanked our path into the city.

"What do you suppose causes those fires?" Heather asked.

"Maybe they're miniature volcanos," I replied.

"Volcanic fires of some sort. Ask David what he thinks."

That evening, we were disappointed to learn that our gorgeous flames were garbage fires at the local dump, the source of the acrid Guayaquil smog.

2. The airport

By five we had immigrated. The others hurried off. I stayed with the gear. That suited me. I wanted to think about being in Ecuador. We had made it. I should be feeling something. But we had so much of our environment with us—clothes, books, ideas, language, smell—that Ecuador felt like Los Angeles.

I was brooding over this when an airport employee spoke to me in Spanish. He seemed to be saying I had a phone call. He kept pointing to another clerk who was holding up a receiver. I didn't know anyone in Guayaquil. I shook my head. He was insistent.

"No, not me." I turned away. I wanted no part of it. I'd been telephone shy since my farewell dinner in a fancy Century City restaurant. On that occasion, I'd been called to the phone by the maitre d' only to be treated to a string of obscenities delivered in a punctilious English accent. I was stunned. The maitre d' apologized and told me he'd had misgivings about giving me the message. I'd annoyed the Englishman who'd been sitting at the next table with my excited chatter about the trip. Apparently this had been his revenge.

That humiliation was fresh in my memory. If I'd offended someone at the Guayaquil airport, I didn't want to know about it. I was shouting "No" again when it dawned on me that I wouldn't understand Spanish obscenities. "Oh, all right. But can you—" I waved vaguely toward the mound of belongings at my feet.

"Sí, señorita," he said, motioning me toward the phone.

A friendly voice greeted me in English. "Welcome to Guayaquil. Are you Heather Simmonds?"

"No, I'm Gwen Moore."

"But you are with her Galapagos party, are you not?"

"Yes."

"I'm the agent in charge of booking the Bronzewing. I've been calling immigration all day, hoping to find you. The crew is waiting for you on Baltra and it's essential that I locate Miss Simmonds—"

"I see your point. I'm not sure, but I think she may be on her way to your office right now."

"That would make sense. We're only ten blocks from the airport. I have the papers for the boat rental for her to sign."

"Really?"

"Is that surprising?"

"It's surprising to be here at all, let alone to have you waiting for us when we arrive. Forgive me, this has been a strange day, and I'm a bit dingy."

"That's understandable. Do you have hotel reservations?"

"No."

"Let me make a couple of suggestions." I wrote down the names of a hotel and several restaurants, each famous for a different kind of atmosphere.

"Thank you so much! You're making it all so easy."

"Glad to be of help. Good luck and success to you in your venture!"

3. A cheap hotel

We regrouped an hour later. Heather had transacted her business with the agent, Pat had changed dollars into sucres, and David and Joe had talked to the powers that be and checked weather. I was surprised to see that they were accompanied by a young man in a threadbare purple shirt.

"Who's he?" I asked.

"An employee, I guess," Joe replied. "He helped us through the maze upstairs."

"He wants a tip," I said.

"I did that. He's being friendly."

I told them about my phone call. "He was so welcoming. Did I tell you he suggested a hotel?" I read the name.

Heather pulled out her Triple-A Guide. "That's rather steep. I can do better than that."

I followed her to the information booth. She picked up the Guayaquil phone book, turned to HOTELS, and started dialing. I listened with awe as she communicated through force of will.

"How much for two rooms?" she asked. "What? No, I want to know how much—mucho—how much mucho for two—dos casas?" she insisted, raising the ante by two decibels.

"You just asked for two houses," I pointed out.

She ignored me. "Two rooms, five people—" she shouted into the receiver.

After twenty minutes of dialing and shouting, she smiled at me triumphantly. "I think I've rented two cheap rooms at the Majestic Hotel."

"Or signed us up for a tour of Venezuela."

"Interesting thought," she laughed. "Now let's find the others and see if they want to rent a car."

The decision didn't come easily, and Joe's patience ran out.

"Forget the car. We'll take a cab."

"But we'd see so much more of the city—"

"We don't have time to get lost in Guayaquil. We're taking a cab."

Joe and Heather were switching roles. Confident and cheerful in his plane, he was cranky on the ground. She was the opposite: eager and aggressive on land, but irritable in the air. They clashed, both places. I wondered how it would be on the boat.

We climbed into the cab and I stopped worrying about them and concentrated on my prayers. Our driver was making good time by ignoring pedestrians, street signs, and an impossible assortment of bicycles, donkey carts, ancient school buses and trucks. I held my breath as he stopped inches from a cart that had pulled in front of us.

It was the first of several near-misses, and I was relieved when we screeched to a halt. We emerged from the cab on what seemed to be the wrong corner.

"This is not a hotel," David said.

"No, wait." Joe pointed to the top of the building. "There's a tiny sign up there that says 'Majestic Hotel'."

The unpretentious lobby was full of South American businessmen. There wasn't a tourist to be seen. And the rooms were ready.

Pat, Joe and I were shown to a large room on the fifth floor. I threw open the French window and looked out at the roof garden across the way. The magnificent cathedral on the corner formed a backdrop for the street scene below.

"Heather's done it again," I said.

"How does she make sign language work over the phone?" Joe asked.

The beds were narrow, but comfortable. The bathroom was strange. You stepped up a foot to enter. It was so small you had to kneel on the toilet to brush your teeth. And the shower nozzle had been installed in the middle of the wall above the long side of the tub. If you didn't pull the curtain before turning on the tap, the water shot across the room to the opposite wall. On the other hand, drainage into the bedroom was good, and the floor could be wiped up quickly. It was ridiculous, but the cold shower felt good, and stretching out on the bed was sheer delight.

By eight-thirty we were clean and hungry. We gathered in the lobby.

"Where to?" I asked. "Shall we take one of the agent's suggestions?"

"Those are tourist traps," David said.

"And we're not tourists?"

"Not his kind of tourist. Let's walk until we see a local restaurant."

"Read 'cheap' for 'local'," Pat commented.

"I may faint from hunger," I mumbled. No one gave a damn.

We had walked only two blocks when we discovered a street lined with restaurants. Tables spilled out onto the sidewalk, creating small islands in the sea of pedestrians.

"Take your choice," Heather said. "There's Japanese, French, Italian—"

"I feel like spaghetti," David said.

"We'll get that on the boat. Let's try the Indian restaurant on the corner."

"I'd rather have Japanese," Joe said. "What do you want, Pat?"

"To sit down."

"How about that steak house in the next block?" David asked.

"What's wrong with Chinese?" Pat pointed to the restaurant behind us.

"Good idea," Joe agreed. "Who's for Chinese?" Joe, Pat and I raised our hands. "Chinese it is."

"This trip would have been impossible with an even number of people," Pat commented.

The menu was in Spanish and Chinese, so we ordered blindly. Our food had just been served when the booking agent and a friend stopped by our table. We found his presence reassuring. We were never quite sure what we were eating, but it tasted marvelous.

"We'll be in the islands at this time tomorrow," Heather announced over coffee.

"If we're not in the ocean," Joe said.

"You can't scare a person who's been living with fear for six months. I'm delighted tomorrow's the day. When we get to the boat, I'm going to sleep for a week."

"Only six hundred and fifty miles of water between us and a good night's rest," David said.

On the way back to the hotel, we mingled with the late evening Christmas shoppers. The festive mood was contagious.

Then our cumulative exhaustion caught up with us and we retreated to our dreams.

5. A bad beginning

I awoke refreshed. I was tired of worrying about the over water hop. Whatever happened today, at least we'd know how it turned out.

"Come on, guys, this is it," I shouted. Neither Joe nor Pat uttered a sound. I tried several more times, but the only response was a low groan from Joe. "If we're going to do it, we have to get a move on."

Receiving no response, I threw on my clothes and hurried to Heather and David's room. I banged on the door and shouted. It seemed a long time before Heather appeared. She was as white as the ruffle on her bonnet. "My God, Heather! Are you sick, too?"

"I'm just a tad tired this morning. Who's sick?"

"Joe and Pat. How's David doing?"

"He's fine. Or at least he will be fine in an hour or so. He has a little headache."

"Time is what we don't have. You people have the fall-aparts. I think we'd better sleep today and fly tomorrow."

"Nonsense. Just give us a few minutes to wake up."

When I returned to the room, Pat and Joe were still asleep. I considered not waking them, but decided against it. If we were really going to fly, Joe needed to get used to the idea. Pat was exhausted, but the others would bounce right back. They were tired and possibly a little afraid. The reality of the over water hop was upon us.

Having decided to press ahead, I shouted and carried on. It wasn't easy. They were hard enough to wake up under the best of circumstances, but this was ridiculous. It was an hour and a half before I had them dressed and propped up on a couch in the fifth floor lobby. They looked miserable.

Heather arrived alone. "David will be along in a minute."

"Meaning?" I asked.

"Meaning he's out of bed." She disappeared only to return ten minutes later.

"Well, where is he?"

"He's brushing his teeth."

"This could take all day," I said.

I sat nervously trying to read the Spanish newspaper while the others dozed. "I think it's about some kind of ship disaster," I announced. "It's either a big ship that went down or a big building that was blown up—"

Heather interrupted me. "He's putting on his trousers. He'll be here momentarily."

When David finally appeared, he was pale and hunched over. I summoned the elevator, then regretted the decision as I watched the four of them file in, looking green. But that was nothing compared to the effect of marching them into the hotel coffee shop.

The waitress brought menus. "You'll feel better if you eat something," I said.

"I'll have toast and coffee," Joe said through clenched teeth.

"Juice," David said.

"That's all?" I asked. "But David, you always—"

"Orange juice."

"How about you, Heather?"

"I think I'll have the toast. I just hope I'll be able to swallow it."

"Pat?"

"Nothing."

"This is not a good beginning, my friends." Not about to be put off by this display of enthusiasm, I studied the menu carefully and ordered tortillas—that sounded like a welcome change from toast—and what I knew to be scrambled eggs. The waitress looked puzzled, but I shrugged it off until she arrived with two plates of eggs: one scrambled, the other a flat omelet.

"Tortilla?" I asked.

She pointed to the omelet. Everyone laughed. I stole some of Heather's toast and ate. The others looked more and more wretched. "Look, guys, be honest," I said. "We're not going anywhere today. Everyone but me is sick, and I can't fly the plane."

"Quit overreacting," David said. "You're making my head throb."

"But there's still so much to do—"

"Yes, that's it. We need a list." Aches and pains wouldn't stop Heather from organizing. "Pat, you're going to stay at the hotel and wait for the agent. He's coming around ten. I told him we'd carry some papers out to our captain. You look as if you could stand a little extra rest. David, you and Joe and I will go on out to the airport, file the flight plan, and get the plane ready. Gwen, you'll go shopping. There are a couple of things we need to buy here in Guayaquil."

"You mean today I don't have to sit and wait? This I will enjoy."

6. *The streets of Guayaquil - II*

My enthusiasm faded when, at eight-thirty, I found myself on a lonely street with my list in hand. It read:
- a long-sleeved shirt for David
- an oil can spout
- a funnel for transferring gas from the five-gallon can into our plastic friend while en route
- toothbrush and comb (Joe had lost his in Panama)
- straw hats for David and Heather

This was my first opportunity to make myself useful, and I was anxious to appear competent. But as I stood on the street corner, my courage almost failed me. I had no idea where the shopping district might be, and not enough Spanish to ask. I picked a direction and started walking, trying to note the names of streets as I passed. But the small signs had been plastered in inconsistent positions on the corners of buildings, and I couldn't spot them all. I was walking east, hoping to find stores nearby.

My nervousness vanished as the early morning street scene caught my attention. There were large, spacious churches at every intersection, all of them crowded with a constant stream of people.

Indians, carrying bundles of handmade serapes on their shoulders, wandered into town to set up displays along the sidewalks. Teary-eyed beggars—children and old people—were already in business, reaching out beseechingly to any likely passersby.

Apparently I looked too ratty to bother with. The beggars let me pass. But others were staring at me. I looked too ratty to be shopping in Guayaquil. My shorts were outrageous for South America, let alone downtown.

It was a great relief to stumble on a dimestore. I sifted through a stack of men's shirts and picked out the largest for David. A little farther down the same street, I found a barber shop with a display of combs in the window. I bought one and was able to negotiate for a toothbrush at the same time. Delighted with my progress, I retraced my route to prove to myself I could find the hotel.

Pat was back in bed. I was glad to see she looked better. She tried to be supportive. "It's wonderful that you found a shirt. But," she pulled it out of its wrapper, "it seems to be short-sleeved, and I think he wants it to protect his arms from the sun."

"I should take it back, shouldn't I?"

"He could use it on cloudy days."

"I can't take it back. I'll never make them understand. I'll buy another one."

Discouraged, I returned to the streets, this time in search of a money exchange. I found the financial district and walked into a bank. The teller spoke English. I told him I was trying to find a funnel and an oil can opener. He wanted to help, but we miscommunicated. For an hour, I wandered in and out of likely looking stores, drawing pictures, creating funnels and oil cans with my hands, using every pantomime gesture I knew. I finally managed to buy a funnel, but no one seemed to have anything remotely resembling an oil can spout.

I was about to give up when an English-speaking business man—complete with briefcase, suit, tie and glasses—came to my rescue. He was charming and funny, and he liked Americans. Especially American women. He wanted to show me the city Saturday night. I thanked him, but explained that we were off to the Galapagos at noon. He inquired about our trip and shook his head in disbelief.

"That's insane. But if there's no talking you out of it, at least let me help you with your shopping. This fellow you need a shirt for. Show me someone about his size." I watched the crowd for a moment before pointing to a large-framed man.

"Got it." He winked at me. "Let's go." He led the way into a department store where he shook hands with the clerk as if they were long lost brothers. He introduced me, then the two of them conversed for another half hour. It seemed a Baroque way to do business, but eventually we emerged, shirt in hand.

Next we determined beyond a doubt that there was no such thing as an American-style oil can spout in Guayaquil. We purchased a beer can opener in its place. Finally we looked at fancy straw hats in a folklore shop. I told him they were too expensive for our needs.

"So we leave at noon—"

"Why are you doing this? There's a charter flight—"

I laughed. "I'm with you. But my friends are adamant. Besides, it's too late to change our plans."

He shook his head. "Assuming you make it, will you call me if—I mean when you return? I would still like to show you Guayaquil."

"That sounds marvelous. Thank you for your help. You've been most generous."

"My pleasure. I wish you the best of luck."

Pat was waiting in the lobby. "The agent brought the papers."

"And you've stopped looking blue. That's a relief."

"I was just tired. Here comes Heather. We're off."

7. The great departure

I felt lighthearted, positively happy, as we retraced our route to the airport. The moment of truth was upon us. In another six hours, all would be known: we would either be on Baltra or in the ocean. And I was tired of worrying about it, one way or the other.

We found the airport contingent in great shape. I stared at the cabin in amazement. Heather and David had redistributed our belongings.

"The emergency landing equipment is on top," Heather explained.

"That's all very well, but you've buried everything else. Where are my books? And what's all this stuff piled on the seats?"

"We have to hold the life jackets in our laps. And we're each responsible for some of the medicine and food we'll need in the life raft. This way, we won't have to go searching."

"You sound as if you expect to crash," I said.

"No, but we do have to be prepared. We only have two minutes to evacuate the plane after it hits the water."

"Don't remind me."

"By the way, the life raft is next to your seat now. Be careful not to lean on it."

"I wouldn't dream of it. Where's our pilot?"

"He and David are doing the flight plan and weather. Here they are now."

Hey, it's nice to see you guys looking human again. I come bearing gifts."

"Like what?"

"Like the funnel for David," I pulled it out of the sack and waved it, "And a beer can opener. There isn't an oil can spout this side of Detroit."

"We don't need it," David said. "I talked an airline mechanic out of his."

"You did what? I spent two hours—"

"The first two hours you ever spent working on this trip," he said. "Quit bitching. We can always use an extra beer opener."

"Joe, what's wrong?" Heather asked. "You look upset."

"Nothing, really. But that's a damned sarcastic bunch they have in the control tower."

"Sarcastic about our plans? You must admit, our plane looks like a toy next to those big babies."

"We don't need a 747 for this trip. Oh God, here comes one of the pilots."

The young man shook Joe's hand. He made a sweeping gesture toward the west. "You're going THERE," then pointed at the plane and said, "In THAT?"

Joe laughed it off, but he looked nervous. "O.K. It's twelve now. If we aren't in the air by one, we don't go today."

"What's the hurry?" I asked. "It's only a five hour flight, and it'll be light well past six."

"That's fine if all goes according to plan. But suppose we miss the islands—"

"What do you mean, 'miss the islands'?"

"I mean I don't want to be flying around out there after dark. There aren't many electric lights on the islands. It's not like looking for New York or Paris."

"I've never heard you sound so pessimistic."

"That's not pessimism, it's realism. Let's get this show on the road."

I squirmed into my seat under my bundle of goodies and fastened my seat belt. A crowd was gathering. Apparently the airline crews had heard about our flight. They were joining the crowd, laughing and talking, and pointing at us. One of them gave me the internationally recognized sign for "loco"—the rotating finger pointed at the head. I grinned and waved.

I spotted Purple Shirt in the crowd. "Heather, look. There's the fellow who helped Joe yesterday."

"He's been around all morning, running errands. Joe overtipped him again. I couldn't persuade him to use sucres and not a five dollar bill."

"He's a nice kid," Pat said. "Let it go."

I laughed. Joe and I argued constantly with David and Heather over tips. Fortunately, Pat is a natural arbitrator.

When I turned back to the gallery, more flight crews had arrived. Everyone was smiling, apparently enjoying our craziness, but I found their presence embarrassing. I wanted to be away from the airport and into our private space in the sky.

Given the external pressure, Joe appeared remarkably calm as he went through the startup procedure. But his poise was shaken when the engine wouldn't turn over. He tried the ignition again and again, each attempt accompanied by a chorus of shouted instructions from the assembled throng.

The members of the gallery pressed around us, vying with each other to give us the benefit of their experience. Since they were all speaking Spanish, it was no help. Purple Shirt managed to force the cockpit window open. He stuck his head inside and jabbered in Joe's face. The confusion was stultifying. I kept thinking the engine would come around, as it had in Santa Monica.

Joe glanced at his watch. "If we're not off the ground in ten minutes, we wait until tomorrow."

He continued his futile attempts until one, then threw up his hands. We all got out, and Joe and David, followed by some of the curious onlookers, walked off in the direction of the local Piper dealer. Only a few of our erstwhile admirers were left to comment as we picked up our bags and headed for the waiting room.

I wandered over to the counter where tickets for the charter flight were sold. The agent spoke English.

"Do you have room for five on tomorrow's flight?"

"Yes, we could handle five more. Do you want tickets?"

"I do, but my friends may not agree. They think we're going to fly a Cherokee-6 out there."

"That's a single engine plane. Tell them that means trouble. A few years ago, a group took off for the islands in a DC-6. They got lost, turned around, and ran out of gas before they made it back here. The whole bunch ended up in life rafts."

"What a great story. I can hardly wait to tell the others."

I returned in time to see the Piper dealer's truck pulling up. Heather and I went out to meet it and followed along behind as the plane was towed to the hanger. The chief mechanic found the problem instantly: fouled spark plugs.

"It could be worse," Heather said. "We could have been stuck at Buenaventura."

I agreed. In the jungle clearing, or on Baltra, it might have taken us days to get help. It had been great luck, if a trifle embarrassing, to have the plane break down in Guayaquil.

Joe emerged from his consultation with the mechanic accompanied by Purple Shirt. We returned to the waiting room. Heather groaned when she saw another fiver change hands.

"Everything is under control," Joe announced. "We'll take off early in the morning. And now," he smiled broadly, "We have a free afternoon in Guayaquil. Anyone for a fancy hotel?"

A simple question, yet it was an hour before we had agreement. There followed yet another ridiculous discussion about rental cars. In an attempt to appease David and Heather, we agreed. But no cars were available at the airport, and we didn't want to wait two hours to get one from town.

8. *The streets of Guayaquil - III*

The delays had left us more irritable than ever. Then the hotel desk clerk wanted to know who was sleeping with whom, and we were in no mood to enlighten him. By the time we got our rooms, our moods had deteriorated still further.

"We're tired and hungry, that's what's wrong," Heather said. "Let's eat in the hotel dining room."

It was on the top floor and commanded a sweeping view of the city. The maitre d's disapproval was clear. But there were no other customers and, at three in the afternoon, there would probably be no new arrivals. He allowed us to sit down.

We selected expensive dishes, and the waiter seemed hesitant about taking our orders. I suppose we looked strange and we were a tad noisy. But he did serve us, and the food was delicious. Pat paid the bill and tip in sucres, and suddenly everyone was all smiles. Perhaps we should have paid in advance. It might have improved the service.

Pat was exhausted, so she went off to lie down. I went to the room with her to be sure she was O.K. She stretched out on the bed her face now a perfect match for the light blue bedspread.

"Are you all right?" I asked.

"Certainly. I just want to rest for a while."

"I talked to the charter flight people. We can still go with them."

"Why would we want to do that?"

"Because this is all so stupid. Don't you see? We almost killed ourselves with a gas leak, and now the plane's acting up. The weather's a disaster, Joe has only flown on instruments once in his life—" I was pacing up and down beside the bed. "What would it take to change your mind?"

"I'm not sure," Pat said. "You see, I really want an adventure. Because I'm sick. Because people keep telling me I can't do anything. And there's something about this flight, taking a small plane and doing something that other people are afraid to do— It's a risk I CAN take, and God damn it, I'm going to do it right."

"All right. I hear you."

"It's different for you. You go ahead on the charter. We'll meet out there later."

"Then I'd have to listen to you guys for the rest of the trip telling me what a great time you had. No, if the Cherokee goes, I'm in it. So, I'm off to find the others. Anything we can bring you?"

"I'm fine."

I found them in the lobby. We were more nervous than tired, and soon discovered that the best way to get rid of excess energy was to have a good fight. Heather was back in rent-a-car mode. She made phone call after phone call, reporting on each in detail. After forty-five minutes, Joe and I were tired of waiting.

"The only way to handle this is to go directly to the rental agency," he said.

"You're absolutely right," I agreed. "Let's do it."

"Hey, David, we're going to rent you a car."

We set off rapidly, enjoying the freedom, feeling clever.

Unfortunately for us, there were no cars available until ten that night.

"How embarrassing," I said as we started back toward the hotel.

"Yeah. We have to tell them. But I don't want to spend the evening with them."

"Let's take a long walk. They won't want to do that."

Heather and David were still in the lobby. They were amused that we had had no luck, and we parted on civil terms. Joe fetched his camera, and we started off through the parks. We gawked at the cathedrals, bought postcards and photographed everything. The streets were alive with after-school children buying sweets from the corner vendors. Old women sat on the sidewalk preparing fires for roasting corn on the cob or frying mush balls. An open butcher stall displayed meat that hung so close to the street it could be poked by passersby. House painters, balanced like acrobats on flimsy bamboo frameworks, splashed bright blues and pinks on building fronts, ignoring the buildings' sides as if working on a movie set.

Tired, we sat down at a sidewalk table and ordered Dos Equis. The ever-sorrowful beggars were a disquieting presence at our elbows.

"They make me uncomfortable," I said.

"But it's their living."

"I know, but I hate it." I took a deep swig of beer before continuing. "Joe, there's something I want to ask you. I know your mind's made up, but I'm curious. Why are you risking your life on this over water hop when there's room for all of us on the charter flight?"

He laughed. "You don't give up easily, do you?"

"Don't you get it? This is really dangerous. The man at the charter flight desk told me a DC-6 had ditched—"

"I heard the same story from the weather guy. Turns out the charter ticket seller didn't tell you the whole story. The plane that ditched was the original charter flight. They got lost. So don't tell me I want to fly with them to be safe." He laughed again.

"That was a rather important detail, wasn't it? But still, Joe, you know the charter is reliable these days. Really, why are you doing this?"

"I'm forty."

"So? Join the club."

"What I mean is, I just noticed I'm forty. I've never stopped being a student. I've worked on campus and made friends with students. The computer's been the center of my life. Flying changed that a little. And then Heather and David came up with this Galapagos trip. It's the most exciting thing I've ever done." He laughed. "I guess, at forty I'm finally learning how to live. Is that a sufficient reason?"

"Quite sufficient."

As darkness fell, the neon lights flashed over our heads, pulsing in time with the noise of the city street. It was like an outdoor nightclub, and we reveled in the heady atmosphere.

9. A good night's sleep

It was after nine when we arrived back at the hotel. "David? Heather? Surely you haven't been here in the lobby all this time?" I said.

"We took a cab back to the airport—"

"What for?"

"To pick up some things we had left in the plane. Anyway, we left Heather's camera in the taxi."

"Oh my God! What are you going to do?"

"We found it. I called the cab company and talked to a few hundred people. They located the driver and he came around with the camera. He just this minute left."

"Did you tip him?"

"You better believe it," David said.

Exulting over this remarkable display of good luck, we tumbled noisily upstairs. Things were going better than we had any right to expect.

But as I was crawling into bed, Joe had another attack of over-excitement.

"I don't feel sleepy. I think I'll wash my clothes."

"What in bloody hell are you talking about? You can't wash your clothes in the middle of the night."

"Why not? If I don't do it now, I'll have to wash them in salt water, and that will make them all stiff and funny."

"If you wash them now, they'll be all damp and funny for the next week. Joe, it's ten. We're getting up at five. That's seven—count them—seven hours."

I couldn't dissuade him, so I tried to sleep while he busied himself with his laundry. He pulled out his travel clothes line and attached one end to the curtain rod, the other to the coat hook on the door.

"You realize that line goes right over Pat's bed, don't you?"

"Can't be helped. That's the only way I can see to support it."

He washed almost everything he had with him, rinsing each garment carefully. He draped the dripping shorts, socks, and shirts, over the line. I had my eyes closed, but the plonk of droplets on the floor suggested he hadn't wrung things out at all. I jumped a foot when Pat shouted:

"It's raining. What the hell is going on?"

"It's only raining in your bed," I replied.

"Sorry, I thought I'd missed you." Joe rushed over and started rearranging his wet clothing.

"I thought I was dreaming, and then I noticed the water running down the sheets."

Joe laughed. "You can thank me for the built-in air conditioning." He handed her a towel.

Pat mopped up as best she could and turned away from the light. I tried to sleep, but he was still rinsing clothes, and I didn't want them hanging over my head. It was after eleven when he finally caved in.

David and I watch as gasoline is funneled from a barrel, through a chamois, into the tanks in Buenaventura, Colombia.

CHAPTER NINE
Ecuador: Guayaquil to Baltra in the Galapagos Islands

1. Second chance

The alarm woke me at five. I stumbled out of bed and ran into a soggy shirt. "Damn it, Joe, your clothes haven't even started to dry." He didn't answer. "I told you it would be like this."

"It's the humidity," Pat mumbled from under her covers. "Probably takes a week to dry anything."

"Hear that, Joe? It's pretty stupid to wash your clothes just before you have to pack them all."

"Do you have to shout?" Pat asked.

"Sorry." I showered and dressed. "Are you people planning to get up?" They ignored me.

I was on my way out the door when Pat screamed, "What in bloody hell—" She had a wet pair of jeans in her face. I'd forgotten the clothesline was attached to the door.

"I'll pull it back up." I closed the door quickly.

David and Heather were already dressed. That was a relief.

And Pat was in the shower when I returned. But it took all four of us to wake Joe. I packed his wet clothes in plastic bags and handed him the dripping bundles. "Your laundry."

He laughed. "Am I supposed to tip you?"

"You're supposed to wake up. We would have left you behind if any of us had known how to fly."

"Lucky me," he replied, laughing again.

We dropped Joe and David at the Piper dealer's and found the coffee shop. I was in a black mood. When they showed up almost immediately, I knew the news was bad.

"They were superb," David said. "The plane's ready."

"It's nice for us they open so early," Pat commented.

"Has anyone checked the gift shop hours? David might be able to find a hat." I cared because he was still wearing mine.

"They're closed until noon."

"What will you do without a hat?" I asked.

"Use yours?"

I glared at him.

"I thought not. I'll improvise."

I tried not to show my relief. "Where's the waitress? I need another cup of coffee."

"Go easy on that stuff," Joe said. "This is a long flight."

"What do you think we've been doing all week? Wearing diapers? You'll like me better after three cups."

2. Boarding

Joe and David were slow with the paperwork. It was almost nine when we crawled into the plane. I was wedged between the life raft and the wall. My lap overflowed with gear that wouldn't fit anywhere else: a life preserver, Joe's oversized jacket, three books, and part of the emergency medical kit. The interior of the plane was never spacious, but today it was claustrophobic. I was nervous. At least our audience outside was smaller and less vocal.

"I talked to the charter flight crew," Joe told me. "They'll be starting out an hour and a half after us. We'll see them overhead somewhere along the way."

"How's the weather?" I asked. "Is this a local storm?"

"Not quite. The clouds extend all the way to the islands."

"Oh, dear God!"

"It's not a problem. There's a radio signal on Baltra. We'll use it to navigate."

"You promised we wouldn't take off if there was a single cloud in the sky."

"Come on, Gwen. It's perfectly safe. We have the Baltra signal, and we'll see the charter flight pass overhead."

"Is Baltra one of the islands?"

"You've really been paying attention, haven't you?"

"It didn't matter until now."

"Baltra's the island we're headed for. In World War II the allies built a landing strip out there."

"So that's why there's a radio signal. Are you sure we can get it?"

"Stop worrying. We will find the signal and Baltra. All will be well. Besides," he laughed, "If we can't find the islands, we'll get to float around in that nice little boat."

3. Over water

It was nine-thirty when we took off, and for the first couple of hours we were caught up in the novelty of being on the final leg of our trip. But the rearrangement of furniture made the life raft a much more prominent design feature, and by twelve it was making me nervous.

"Who's going to inflate the raft if we crash?" I shouted at Joe over the roar of the engine. The racket was incredible, but it was a sound I had come to love, especially now that we were four hundred miles from the mainland.

Joe turned sideways in his seat. "Not crash, Gwen. Ditch. Planes are ditched."

"Well, pardon my stupidity. So if we ditch the plane, who's going to inflate the raft?"

"David's in charge of the raft. He'll have to move fast. Once we're down, we have two minutes to get out."

I searched his face for clues to our fate. He looked worried. "Thanks for the words of cheer."

"It happens to be a matter of life and death." He returned to the controls.

I looked back at my companions. Pat was engrossed in her book. Heather was struggling with air sickness. "You O.K.?" I asked.

"No," she replied.

"Did you hear Joe? He's not usually so uptight."

Heather wet her lips. "He has a lot on his mind."

"Do you honestly think we could miss the islands?"

"Yes. That's why we brought the raft."

"Have you tried inflating it?"

"Once, in the apartment. It was a bitch."

"That's so reassuring." I turned around and punched Joe in the back. "We need to talk about this two minute evacuation. In case you've forgotten, Heather can't swim."

David slapped the map in his lap. "You bet your sweet ass we haven't forgotten. I'll go back there and open her door."

"You're going from the right front seat to the left rear door? How?"

"I'll crawl."

"Over me?"

"How else? I have to be back there, anyway. I'm the only one who's ever inflated the raft."

"Just a minute here," Joe interrupted. "I'm in charge of evacuation. I'll get out first, through my door. Gwen," he looked back at me, "You will pass the life raft up to David. He will hand it to me. We'll inflate it on the wing."

"No way," David objected. "Heather needs my help. Besides, the raft has to be inflated inside the plane."

That caught Pat's attention. "You won't be able to get it out the door."

"Damn it, I'm in charge of the raft. We'll do it my way."

Heather poked my shoulder. "Tell them I'll get my own self out of here. I'll climb on the wing and wait there. I don't want to sit inside a sinking plane."

That seemed sensible to me, but not to David. "I refuse to sit idly by while you flounder around in the open sea. I will crawl over Gwen and open the back door."

"That could take the whole two minutes," I said. "Let's change seats right now."

"Good thinking. You go back with Heather, and I'll—"

"Hold on just a damn minute," Joe shouted. "There will be no musical chairs aboard this aircraft."

"It was just an idea—"

"Forget it."

I glanced at Pat. Only the top of her head was visible. She had returned to her book. I retreated, too. The window offered no relief: clouds stretched for miles in all directions, a vivid reminder of our predicament.

"Joe, tell me we don't need to worry about this. We're on course, right? You're getting the signal from Baltra?"

"No."

"What do you mean, 'no'?"

"I mean I can't pick up the signal."

"Did you plan this trip as the final test for your instrument training?"

"Right." He laughed.

I didn't think it was funny. I stared at our polyethylene friend. He was by now a member of the group. Some days his expression seemed pleasant, even friendly. Today he looked sinister, his plastic top slammed down over his head. But his expression didn't bother me. It was his empty condition. It reminded me that we were nearing the point of no return.

As if tuning into my thoughts, Joe swiveled around and said, "We made it. There's no turning back now."

"I know Pat would love to arrive in Baltra on a raft, but I thought a pilot would have more sense."

Joe laughed.

I leaned forward to peer at the gas gauges. Two of the tanks were registering twenty gallons, one was at fifteen, the fourth at ten. And we had five more gallons in the red can at my feet. At about eighteen gallons per hour— "You're wrong, Joe. We could go back. We have four hours' worth of gas left."

"We're doing better than I expected. But the gauges aren't accurate. It would be risky to return, even now. The good news is, we have plenty of time to search for the islands if we miss them the first time around."

"Damn, he makes me nervous," I said to Heather.

"I have an idea. Let's feed the extra five gallons to our friend here."

"Great. I need to move."

Our first problem was the stuff we were holding. There was no place to stow it. Pat offered her lap. We buried her under our excess gear and stood up. By climbing on my seat, I was able to pry open the tank lid. Heather is two inches shorter than I. She had to stand on tiptoe to insert the funnel.

"Damn!" she said. "It's almost touching the ceiling."

"We can't pour anything into that," I said.

"Maybe we can tip the funnel."

Pat was watching us. "It won't work."

It didn't seem likely to me, either, but Heather was the one with a Ph.D. in chemistry and a lab full of complex equipment. Who was I to argue? We hoisted the gas can to the edge of the tilted funnel and started to pour. The arrangement was precarious, but we might have managed if the plane had held steady. It didn't. Some of the gas flowed down the outside of the tank. The rest trickled down our arms and onto our shirts. None went inside. We were laughing so hard we almost spilled the whole can. Finally we had it wedged back in place on the floor.

"I told you it wouldn't work," Pat said.

Heather struggled into her seat. "It was worth it just to move."

But Joe wasn't pleased. "What the bloody hell are you fools doing? Haven't you learned anything? You cannot slop gas around the cabin!"

That sounded ridiculous to me. "Everybody gets to spill gas once on this trip. This was our turn."

"It's not funny."

"Only your mistakes are funny." I turned to Heather. "I guess we can't use the gas from the can."

"We could pour it into the funnel with the drinking cup."

"What if someone wants a drink of water afterwards?"

"A little flavoring isn't going to hurt."

I leaned over to get my gear from Pat and was nauseated by the smell of gas on my arms. I opened the Ricas crackers Joe and I had purchased on our walk and handed them around. They tasted like graham crackers soaked in gasoline. That didn't help my mood. Neither did the weather: it was still clouds, clouds, clouds in all directions.

4. Finding our way

I was more uncomfortable than afraid. My fear had settled in my stomach like a chunk of cement. I found a book in my lap and propped it open with Joe's jacket. It was Timothy Leary's JAIL RECOLLECTIONS. I was going to love that one on the raft.

Eventually I gave up trying to read and checked my watch. It was two thirty-nine. We had been in the air for five hours. If we were on course, we would be landing on Baltra in a few minutes.

"Joe, we're almost there, aren't we?"

"No." He turned to look at me.

"But it's been five hours."

"What? That was an estimate. It'll be a while."

I wondered if he had any idea where we were. If he was lost, we'd be floundering in the Pacific Ocean. I shuddered. "Heather, do you remember what Lieutenant Moreno told us? There's no search and rescue in South America."

Pat looked up from her book. "That wasn't news. In case you haven't noticed, Joe always has the only copy of the flight plan."

"That's right," Heather agreed. "He has to present it at the next airport."

"Wonderful," I said. "If we go down, we may be in for a long ride in our little raft. Why does that bother me?"

"I can't imagine," Pat replied.

Heather poked my arm. "I'm just as scared as you are."

"It would be quite an experience, landing on the ocean," Pat commented. "One group floated around this area in a life boat for a hundred and eight days before being picked up."

I made a rapid calculation. "Fifteen and a half weeks? Good Lord, do we have enough food?"

"Just look at all this stuff." Heather waved her hand toward the food box.

I glanced at the limp body of the life raft. I wasn't supposed to lean on it. That worried me. If it couldn't support my elbow, how could it handle five people on the open sea? Finding no solace in the conversation, I pretended to return to my reading. Actually, I was making a decision: I would take as many books as I could carry when we evacuated. I did not want to float around listening to David and Heather.

"Ask Joe if we'll be able to see the Galapagos volcanos through the clouds?" Heather said.

"It all depends," he replied. "Right now, I think they're covered."

For a few minutes we lapsed into silence. My thoughts wandered. I squirmed and almost screamed. My right leg was asleep and did not appreciate being disturbed. The pain was excruciating. I tried to concentrate on something else.

Heather was sitting on the edge of her seat, clutching binoculars and scanning the horizon. Suddenly, she jumped up, sending an avalanche of gear to the floor. "Look, over there. Isn't that a peak? Could the islands be there, on the horizon?"

"You're pointing north, Heather. If your cloud bank is over the islands, we're a long way off course—"

"What's going on back there?" David asked.

"Heather thinks that cloud bank on the right is a volcano."

"Hand me the glasses." He peered through them for several minutes. "I see it!" He opened his map to check the positions of the island volcanos. "There's no doubt about it. Joe, have a look. Here." He pushed the glasses into his hands.

After a brief look, Joe shrugged. David turned to me. I tried to focus the glasses, but wasn't surprised when I saw nothing but clouds.

"Did you see it?" he asked.

"Yes," I replied, not wanting to argue. "It's fantastic." I passed the glasses back to Pat.

"Joe, you'd better throw a right," David said. "We're going away from the islands."

Joe looked at him in amazement. "You're out of your mind."

I breathed a sigh of relief. At least he wasn't going to start chasing a mirage around the Pacific.

But David was sure he was right, and Joe's refusal to change direction spurred him on. "You see them, don't you, Pat? They're at three o'clock."

"There's nothing there that even remotely resembles a mountain peak."

"For God's sake, you're looking in the wrong place. We're going to go right past the islands and end up in the middle of nowhere." He buried his nose in his map.

I was delighted that Joe was ignoring phantom islands, but I wasn't finding his behavior exactly reassuring. He seemed engrossed in switching from one radio station to another.

"Haven't you made contact with Baltra yet?" I asked.

"No luck," he replied, continuing to play with the knobs.

Obviously, he didn't know where we were. This could be it.

There are some advantages to being an all-out pessimist. Since I had always expected the worst, I wasn't as upset as Heather and David. Joe seemed more excited than worried. Pat was content.

She looked forward to an emergency landing on the ocean. That was something she'd never done.

My position in the middle seat put me farthest from the doors. This was beginning to concern me. I decided to give the landing procedures one last try. "I don't care what the plan is, guys, but there has to be one. As things are, you'll be so busy arguing, you'll forget to open the doors."

"It's all set," David assured me. "I told you. I'll climb over you and help Heather—"

"You'll do no such thing—"

"I'm in charge of this plane and—"

David stopped the argument. "Now it's absolutely clear. Joe, you've got to make a forty five degree turn to the right."

Joe ignored him. David tried again. "Look over there. That's the top of Alceda. You've got to turn, man—"

Joe studied the map David handed him, then stared through the glasses at the mountain-shaped cloud.

"You're right." He turned the plane toward the cloud.

I was stunned. "Don't do it, Joe. It's a cloud."

He ignored me. We were lost.

I wondered what the ocean looked like beneath the heavy layer of clouds. I glanced over David's shoulder. We had at least two hours' worth of gas left. If the islands were close, we would have time. But we must stay calm.

I stared down at the impenetrable fluff. Suddenly we came upon a break in the clouds. To my astonishment, I could see the ocean and a small patch of land. I shouted: "There it is, right there. We made it. That's land down there."

The clouds continued to break up, uncovering a flat, brown surface that grew into an island before our eyes. It looked remarkably inviting. That is to say, it looked solid.

As we passed the tip of the island, a large rock formation came into view, jutting out of the water like a knife. "That's Kicker Rock," Heather exclaimed. "It's the landmark at the end of San Cristobal."

"We're back on the map." David pushed my hat back in a gesture of relief.

Joe headed down through the remaining clouds, and the entire scene opened up. We could see for miles. Pat spotted Hood and Floreana, two of the outlying islands, far to the south. Elated, Joe set his course for Baltra.

I was thankful we had found the Galapagos, but I would have been equally happy to see the coast of South America. Or even Scotland.

Frigate birds circle overhead as Hugo cleans fish for ceviche.

CHAPTER TEN
Baltra to Plazas

1. The Welcome

"There's the Bronzewing," Heather yelled in my ear.

"What makes you so sure?" I asked.

"It's the only boat in the bay. It has to be ours."

"Let's go down and find out." Joe reached for the radio.

"We have lots of gas," David said. "We could have a look around before we land."

I appealed to Pat and Heather. "Tell him he's crazy."

"It's a great idea," Pat said.

Heather made a face. "I'd rather find the ladies loo."

"I'm with you," I said. "Joe, where are you going?"

"To James Island. It's straight ahead."

Pat had told me the Galapagos resemble the Hawaiian Islands, so I expected a tropical paradise. Instead, James was desolate. Muted sunlight blazed on white sand, its fire reflected from volcanic slopes. Vegetation was sparse and dry.

"Isabella's close," David consulted his map. "Let's have a look."

"While we're at it, why not do the Falklands?" I asked.

"Enough of this," Joe said. "We're going in."

Baltra looked as uninviting as James. No one else seemed to notice. They must have known all along. We had risked our necks to reach a desert.

"Did you ask for a reception committee, Heather?" I asked.

"No, a bathroom. Their English must be lousy."

"Joe, who are those people in uniform?"

"Ecuadorian military." He parked as directed, and we struggled out. The excited strangers shook our hands and babbled in Spanish. I noticed a tall, sunburned Englishman in the group.

"None of you speaks Spanish?" he asked.

I shook my head.

"These men are in charge of the landing strip. I'll translate."

I laughed. His ancient jeans, sandals, and T-shirt made him a perfect spokesman for us.

He turned to Joe. "You're the pilot, aren't you?" Joe nodded. "They say, 'Welcome and congratulations'."

"Thank them for us, will you?" Joe replied.

"They want me to tell you that they are very impressed. Only one other single engine plane has made this trip. That was some famous woman aviator, many years ago."

Embarrassed, Joe laughed and shook their hands again.

"Who was it?" Pat asked. "Beryl Markham? Amelia Earhart?"

"They don't remember the woman's name," he replied. "Your gasoline has been delivered. Those two barrels over there."

"I can't believe what you've done, Heather," I said. "You made it happen—the gas, the boat—"

"That's all very well, but we seem to be missing our crew."

"Sorry, love." The Englishman turned to her. "I should have introduced myself. I'm your captain, Peter Stapley."

One of the Ecuadorians grabbed his shoulder.

"Sí, sí," Peter said. "Uno momento— They need your landing papers."

Heather pulled a bundle from her oversized purse. "Everything's there—the permit to land on Baltra, the national park permit, all the papers we were told to file."

"Here's my contribution," Joe said. "The flight plan."

The Ecuadorians seemed delighted with these offerings, but continued to press for details of the flight: the weather, the gas, the route. After each explanation, they would exclaim again that it was an astonishing feat.

Joe basked in the attention.

2. The crew

"I hate to break this up," Peter said, "but we must reach Plazas by dusk." He spoke to the Ecuadorians.

"Sí, sí." The man in charge turned his attention to the papers in his hand and talked rapidly.

"Oh, God," Peter said. "Something's wrong with one of your documents— Wait. It's O.K. He says your flight was so impressive, he's not going to quibble over details. George, come meet the people. George is your guide. And this is Hugo. He's our cook."

We shook hands with a sad-eyed American kid and a plump, smiling brown man. "I'm Gwen—"

"Hugo doesn't speak English," Peter said. "Try sign language. Now about your luggage—"

"Peter, I don't understand," Heather said. "We decided not to have a guide."

"You don't get to decide."

"Since when?"

"Since the Galapagos became a National Park. Now everybody gets a guide."

"If we'd known, we would have asked Tui de Roy. I talked to her when she was in California—"

"Keep it down," David said. "George will hear you."

"He already did," George replied. "I'm afraid you're stuck with me. Tui knows more, but she's busy this week."

"I didn't mean that the way it sounded—"

"No problem."

"About your luggage—" Peter said.

"We'll have to do a quick sort."

We hurried to the plane. Joe and David pulled the life raft and camping gear onto the ground. I shoved my books into my duffel bag and picked up my snorkeling gear. David and Heather couldn't find their bags. I walked to the edge of the bluff and faced into the strong, sea-scented wind. It was refreshing, almost cold. I closed my eyes and let it clear the cobwebs from my brain.

"Gwen, help me put the raft back," Joe called. "Will we need the fire extinguisher?"

"For God's sake, Joe. Of course not."

Peter picked up my duffel bag and started off toward an ancient vehicle. "The bus is leaving," he said.

Joe locked the plane and pocketed the key. We shook hands with our military friends and followed Peter. A new chapter in our journey had begun.

3. The dock

The "bus" was a flat bed truck with a few randomly placed metal hoops and no seats. It resembled a motorized covered wagon. I jumped on and grabbed a hoop overhead. The gears crashed and we lurched forward onto a bumpy dirt road. I stared at the barren terrain. It was more hostile than I'd imagined. This was going to be three weeks of unrelieved boredom. I was in a foul mood when the bus jolted to a stop.

"Everybody out," Peter yelled.

I picked up my purse and jacket and stumbled down. We were next to a massive dock, but no boat was in sight. "Where's the Bronzewing?" I asked.

"Forty feet down." Peter pointed to the water.

"That miniscule boat down there?"

"Gwen," Heather said, "you know perfectly well the Bronzewing is a forty-eight foot sloop."

"Forty-eight feet sounded a lot bigger in the brochure."

"It's all a matter of perspective," she replied.

"Actually," Peter said, "this dock was built for large cruisers. That makes all the small boats look tiny. But it works. See how close the driver got to the rope ladder?"

"Ladder?" I said. "You mean that ... that thing dangling down the side of the pier?"

"Right. That ladder takes you to the lower dock."

"You'll have to help Pat," Heather said. "She's not well."

"You didn't tell me anyone had health problems," Peter snapped.

"You didn't tell us about the rope ladder," Heather replied.

"I'm not sick. I'm tired." Pat started down the ladder.

"But your face, Pat. You're turning blue—" Heather sounded alarmed.

"It's the sun," Pat replied. "I don't tan, I blue."

"At least let me take the camera," I said.

"I have it."

We watched her for a moment, then I grabbed my things and started after her. I was almost down when David shouted, "Hold it, Gwen. We're going to pass the gear down."

David positioned himself halfway down, Joe toward the top. Peter passed the bags down from the top. Our system was efficient, and we soon had the luggage in yet another pile on the lower dock. Our little group gathered around Peter with all the nervousness of a newly-formed tourist group.

4. *The Bronzewing*

Hugo loaded the dinghy, and soon the raucous outboard motor announced his first round trip. I looked at the Bronzewing. She was bouncing jauntily on the waves, proud of her freshly painted brown and white markings. She looked friendly, but decidedly small. The others were making yet another set of plans.

"Heather, you and I will go on the next trip," Peter said. "There's a problem with the itinerary you requested."

"We need Pat. We planned it together."

"What's wrong with it?" Pat asked.

"For starters, we'd be going against the current."

"So we'll go the other way," Pat said.

"Good. That means there isn't time to go to both of the outlying islands. You'll have to choose between Tower and Hood."

"Let's give up Tower," Pat said.

"I'd rather go there and miss Hood," Heather said. They were still arguing when Hugo picked them up.

Eventually Hugo returned for the rest of us. When we reached the Bronzewing, he climbed onto the deck and held the dinghy close to the side. I struggled over the rail. He shouted at me in Spanish and pointed at my feet. Obediently I removed my shoes.

One by one, we made our way into the compact head, then stumbled topside to enjoy the view. Peter emerged from the cabin to take charge. "There are three sleeping areas on board," he said. "The room at the foot of these steps is for the crew. Hugo and I have the bunks, George sleeps on deck."

I watched him as he talked. Despite his youth, his shoulders were stooped like an old man's, as if he had been overworked for years. I relaxed when it dawned on me that, for the next nineteen days, Peter, not I, would be in charge of getting people out of bed.

"There are two berths in the bow," he went on. "It's private, but the movement of the boat is intensified. It can make you sick. Then there are four bunks, two up, two down, on either side of the table in the center of the boat. Take your choice. We're late. Hugo!" he pointed to the anchor.

"Heather, you and David take the forward berths," I said. "It's at least got some privacy."

"Heather will get sick," Pat said.

"Nonsense," David said. "We won't be traveling at night."

"George, fix these people some lunch," Peter said.

"We don't eat lunch," Joe said.

"It's after three," Heather said. "Dinner will be soon."

"Dinner might be too late. We'll be hitting heavy currents, and I don't want anyone to get seasick."

It seemed natural to be taking orders from Peter. Perhaps it was the T-shirt. We marched below. Joe, Pat and I threw our bags in the upper bunks and collapsed on the lower ones that doubled as seats for the foldout table. The galley and eating area were all business except for a small painting above the table. It showed a Bronzewing duck, it's brown and white markings reminiscent of the fresh paint on our boat. It was a nice touch, and I was already sorry I wouldn't get to meet Julian Fitter, the Englishman who had sailed the Bronzewing out from England.

5. Our first ride

George was standing at the head of the table. That put him in the galley. He passed us bread, peanut butter, cheese, bananas, and cookies while heating water on the tiny gas stove. The Horniman's tea led to a round of bad jokes. Then we fell silent. We were still lingering over our tea when the motor started.

"Aren't we going to sail?" I asked.

"No. The currents in the Galapagos are powerful, and we have a lot of miles to cover in a short time."

"Damn! I thought the whole point was to sail."

"You could. It would lengthen the trip by about two weeks, but if you have the time and money—"

"No way. Heather, you said we'd be sailing—"

"I said we'd be in a sailboat, and we are." She smiled.

"Look at the good side," David said. "We're already accustomed to screaming at each other over the engine."

When we returned to the deck, we were well into the channel between Baltra and the larger Santa Cruz. The ocean was quiet, held firmly in place by these two stolid land masses. Sailing would have been marvelous. I looked back at Santa Cruz.

"I don't believe it," I said. "Trees."

"You weren't expecting trees?" Peter asked.

"Not after Baltra. That has to be the ugliest island in the entire world."

"It wasn't always that way. An American Army Air Corps unit was stationed there during World War II. They killed most of the vegetation. They also systematically shot all the animals."

"My God, that's disgusting!"

"And human."

I joined the others, who were exploring the bow.

"Would you believe this fruit?" David pulled a banana from a long spike lashed to the mast.

At the end of the channel, we had a spectacular view of Baltra's underpinnings. Gray rock, arranged in precise slanting patterns, rose several hundred feet above the water. The massive wall was covered with hundreds of leafless grey trees.

"George, those trees look like ghosts. Are they dead?"

"No. The Palo Santo trees are bare most of the time. Once a year they turn green overnight. When they flower, the aroma is so strong you can smell it for miles."

"How are they distributed?" David asked.

"Distributed?" George questioned.

"Yes. Which islands do they occur on?"

"I've seen them on most of the islands."

"Is there just one variety?"

"What is this, twenty questions?" I asked.

"If that's what it takes, yes."

"You can analyze things to death, David."

"Don't you want to understand this place?"

"Not like that, I don't." I moved back to the cockpit. I sat down across from Peter and watched the shadows fall on the graceful Palo Santo trees. The gray-on-gray was interrupted by clumps of low-growing, dull-green cacti. "So even Baltra has its magnificence. I had written it off."

"That's part of the fascination. Just when you think you understand how it is, you find a contradiction. It's a hard place to leave. I'll never make it back to England."

The open sea seemed relatively calm. Then, without warning, a huge wave slopped heavily over the side, soaking us. It was fun for everyone except Pat. She had been sitting on the bow, waiting for the perfect shot of Santa Cruz. She rushed below to dry her camera. The others joined us in the cockpit. We were crowded, but comfortable.

"How far to Plazas?" David asked.

"It's a short drive. We should be there in an hour."

6. Parked at Plazas

Peter anchored in a quiet bay in time for a spectacular sunset over the top of the tiny island.

"Sorry about the drinks. It's warm rum and grapefruit juice. No ice on this boat."

"You think we'd notice?"

"Most people do. They seem to miss that more than showers." .

"Are you kidding? Who cares! God, this place is magical."

We fell silent, gently rocked by the boat. The sea was calm, and, when the sun disappeared, a large moon took its place, painting a silvery gold path across the water. I felt my fears dissolving. I could forget about flying for now.

Peter stuck his head out of the cabin. "Dinner's ready. Hope you don't mind spaghetti. We'll do better after tonight."

George and Peter sat with us on the bunks, so we were four on one side, three on the other. Hugo preferred the steps at the far end of the galley. Since this was a small area, he was still part of the group.

"Hugo, the spaghetti." I gestured toward the plate. "Magnifico!"

He flashed me a smile.

"You people are a relief," Peter said. "We had assumed you were jet setters, and we were sure you wouldn't be happy with the

Bronzewing. But we knew as soon as we heard your motor. And were we ever glad to hear that motor."

"Did you think we were lost?" Joe asked.

"I know you were lost, Joe." I glanced at Heather who nodded. "He spent the time tuning the radio, looking for the Baltra signal."

Joe laughed. "I was navigating. I used two radio stations on the mainland to figure out where we were."

"Why didn't you tell me?"

"You didn't ask. How long have you been waiting, Peter?"

"Two days. We were a tad concerned."

"When we spotted the plane," George said, "we rushed over in the dinghy and found the bus people. We all drove to the air-strip. We get there, and all the military types are jabbering away at us, and you've vanished."

"We weren't gone long," Joe said.

"Long enough to scare us."

"Hugo's laughing. You said he didn't speak English."

"He doesn't. But he may well understand it. Are you folks from Los Angeles?"

"Except for Heather, yes. You know she's English?"

"I did notice a slight accent."

"How about you, George? Where are you from?"

"Nebraska. Omaha, Nebraska."

"Are you down here studying?" Heather asked.

"I wish I were. No, I'm down here because of the war."

"He's a draft dodger," David said.

"Conscientious objector," I said.

"David's right. I don't want to fight in Vietnam."

"I don't see David volunteering." I bit my tongue.

"Our country never gets into unfortunate wars like that, right, Heather? So tomorrow we see Plazas." Peter kept the conversation on the islands until we were nodding. It was only eight, but it had been a long day.

"I'm going to bed," David announced.

"Great idea. I'm first in the head." I fumbled in my duffel bag for my pajamas. They weren't there. Then I remembered. I had been so busy packing Joe's laundry, I had left my lounging pajamas in the bathroom. What an idiot! They were the most presentable clothes I had with me. I had enjoyed the contrast with Heather's white longies. I wouldn't be showing off anymore.

I had two options: I could wait until the lights were out and disrobe in the dark, or climb into bed and pull my clothes off there. I decided to wing it upstairs. I stood on Joe's bunk and hoisted myself up. It wasn't easy. The ceiling was only two feet from the mattress.

Squirming out of my jeans was a challenge. Exhausted, I kicked the wad of clothes to the end of the bunk and closed my eyes. The boat was rocking gently. I thought I'd fall asleep immediately. But I was still high from all the excitement.

Yoga didn't help. I jammed my toes against the pipes that ran along the ceiling. I fell asleep trying to remember where the aspirin was. Almost immediately I was awakened by a loud bang. My unfortunate habit of sitting up to turn over was my undoing.

My head had hit the ceiling hard. This was a rotten set up. But I didn't have long to worry. The blow left me dazed. I slept as if I'd been drugged.

CHAPTER ELEVEN
Plazas to Barrington

l. Morning in the Galapagos

The whistle of a tea kettle woke me. I heard Peter whisper to Hugo in Spanish, then shoes scraping on the steps. It was five-thirty. I peered over the edge of the bunk. Pat and Joe were sleeping soundly. This was my chance. I turned onto my stomach and slipped my legs over the side. My toes found the wooden edge of Joe's bunk. He didn't stir. I grabbed my duffel bag and dashed into the head to dress.

The tea kettle was still steaming. I fixed a cup of instant and joined Peter and George in the cockpit.

"What a beautiful sunrise," I said. "Everything looks new."

"The ocean's unusually calm this morning," Peter replied. "How did you sleep, love?"

"Well, thank you. There's something about the rocking of the boat—"

"The old 'back to the womb' ploy," Peter commented.

"Is that a radio?"

"It's Hugo. He always sings when he swabs the deck."

"It's a happy sound. What's he singing about?"

"You don't want to know." He eyed my shorts. "You're going to have to cover up."

"Because of Hugo? You're joking."

He laughed. "No, because of the sun. It's rays are intensified on the equator. You're fair. You could burn to a crisp."

Peter's sun-bleached hair stuck out from under his sailor hat. His nose and cheeks were already thick with zinc oxide. "You're a fine one to talk. You're a walking burn victim if I ever saw one."

"Precisely. Do you want this to happen to you? Good morning, Pat."

"I'd say hello, but you look grim," I said.

"I'm fine." Pat slumped onto the seat with her coffee. The others were slow to surface and equally enthusiastic.

Heather and David didn't appear until almost eight. Peter and Hugo went below to fix breakfast. It was elegant—scrambled eggs, toast, cereal, papaya.

"My God, that was fantastic," David exclaimed.

"I'm disappointed," I said. "You guys promised me K-Rations. I planned to lose ten pounds."

"I don't see what you're complaining about." Heather sounded annoyed. "You eat more than I do, and you don't gain weight."

"I don't eat Hershey bars, Heather. It makes a difference if you eat Hershey bars."

"Here's what we do today." Peter perched awkwardly on the steps in the galley. "This morning you'll have a look at Plazas. Hugo will run you over in the dinghy. George will be there to answer your questions. Immediately after lunch we leave for Barrington."

"We're tired," I protested. "Why not stay one more night and enjoy this gorgeous place?"

"You're forgetting the schedule," Heather reminded me. "If we don't keep moving, we'll miss some of the best places."

"THE SCHEDULE," I said. "Damn, I keep forgetting we're on a scientific expedition."

"You needn't be sarcastic."

"So is everybody ready? The dinghy leaves in five minutes. Protect yourself from the sun."

"David, we must do something about your face—" Heather said.

"Would you like a suggestion?" I ducked.

"No, I would not." David and Heather disappeared behind the curtain that separated the head and their berths from our area.

"Gwen, can I borrow some zinc oxide?" Joe asked.

"Alright, but I want it back by noon."

2. Plazas

Pat, Joe and I were eager to see Plazas. Hugo and George lowered the dinghy from it's traveling position high up on the stern, and Hugo drove us across.

"You're looking at an enormous volcano," George shouted over the roar of the outboard motor. "Most of it's under water."

The visible portion was not much bigger than a football field—perhaps half again as long—rising to a point. The slope was draped in a radiant red ground cover, interrupted by a scattering of trees and cacti.

Hugo drove us to the designated landing spot on an outcropping of rocks. We were greeted by four tame land iguanas, all over six feet long. Their eyes were large and intelligent, dark against golden, iridescent skin. They seemed as interested in us as we were in them.

"George, why aren't they afraid?" Joe asked.

"There are so few predators, they have nothing to fear. That's true of most animals in the Galapagos."

"This is the way it must have been in the Garden of Eden," Pat said. "Before man discovered greed."

The iguanas and the people sat down and stared at each other. I was touched by their vulnerability and their curiosity about us. We stayed with them a long time.

"What do you suppose is keeping Heather and David?" George asked. "It's been thirty minutes."

"They're having trouble getting organized," I replied. "David never did buy a hat."

"Here they come," Joe said.

We walked down to the landing to greet them. "My God!" Pat exclaimed. "Do you see what I see? David's wearing Heather's bonnet."

I stared at David as he came ashore. "You look stunning."

"You have enough gear to camp out," Joe said.

"We weren't sure what we'd need." Heather replied. "I see you've found some land iguanas. What do they eat, George?"

"They're vegetarians. They feed on the low growing plants. Speaking of their eating habits, I can show you a bit of evolution right here. The iguanas like the cactus flowers and leaves. These plants have evolved a protective cover. See this? It's almost a bark."

"It looks like a sugar pine," Pat said.

"The imitation bark works. Now the iguanas get the occasional fallen flowers as a treat, and the plants survive."

"So these poor fellows just sit here and dream."

"Once in a while a misguided tourist does this." George picked a yellow bud from the cactus and offered it to one of the golden creatures. "You can't do this, by the way. It's illegal."

The iguana was mad with happiness. Pieces of yellow flower dripped from his lips as he chomped it thoroughly. "Our first example of adaptation to coexistence in the islands." Heather was pleased. "Tell me about this red ground cover."

"It resembles iceplant. The foliage has a green phase as well as this red one. The bloom is yellow."

"So the red effect is from a leaf, not a flower. What's the scientific name?"

"I don't know."

"David, where's that book?" David set the knapsack on a rock and pulled out a heavy volume. We left the two of them pouring over it, and walked on up the slope.

We stopped to talk to another group of friendly iguanas. Joe touched my arm. "Look behind you. The ocean is incredible."

"It's almost as if we're seeing over the horizon," Pat said.

Heather and David caught up with us. "It's *Portulaca lutea*," he told us.

"What is?" I asked.

"The ground cover."

"I feel so much better knowing that." My sarcasm was a mistake, but I couldn't seem to shut up. I hurried on up the slope. I was curious about the other half of the island. To my surprise, it didn't exist. I was at the edge of a cliff, looking down five hundred feet into jagged rocks and thrashing ocean. I was still standing there when the others came along.

"George, you should have warned me. I could have gone right over the edge."

"Wouldn't be the first time. You are standing on an over-hanging cliff. Every once in a while, part of it gives way. We noticed it last year when one of the guides rode it down."

"Was he hurt?"

"Yes. He broke his leg, and was badly shaken up. But he was lucky. It would be easy to kill yourself on those rocks."

"Is this the result of an eruption?" David asked.

"Yes. Plazas is a fragment of an old volcano. The exposed cliff provides nesting spots for a variety of birds. You can see from the way they're circling how the currents swirl against the rocks. This is a marvelous place to fly."

Birds were everywhere: above us, below us, rising and falling as they rode the wind currents.

"There's our first boobie bird." Pat pointed to a nest on a rocky outcropping close to the top of the cliff.

"Those are, obviously, the masked boobies," George said.

"What else could you call a white bird with a black mask?" I said.

"It's the Neanderthal brows that get me," Pat commented.

"Between that and the crossed golden eyes, they look like a gang of insane robbers."

"I don't see how they can fly," David said. "They're so big and awkward, they shouldn't be able to get any lift."

"Watch for a minute. They're awkward on land, but beautiful in the air. They do need room for take off, though. Look, there's the tropic bird. That one you won't see often."

The small, trim bird was all white except for sharp black eyes and a red beak. In flight, the two-foot tail feathers sailed behind him like a piece of silk. He flew with a curious knowing movement, as if the world had been designed to his specifications.

David had Heather's camera. He was standing at the edge of the cliff, focusing on the proliferation of nests on the steep escarpment. "What f setting do you have, Pat?"

"I used f4.5. But don't go by that. My light meter's been

strange lately. There must be a NO VACANCY sign up here. I don't see any empty nesting spots."

"You're right about that," George agreed. "There are baby birds of all descriptions and ages. Gulls, boobies, tropic birds—"

"How do these species stand being so close together?" I asked. "Don't they fight all the time?"

"Not in the Galapagos. They can't afford to be fussy with nesting space so limited."

"So the ones who survive are the ones who learn how to ignore each other?"

"Right. Let's go visit the sea lions. They're sunning themselves on the rocks down there."

"This island's amazing," I said. "It's tiny, but there's so much going on."

The marine iguanas were wonderful dark, wrinkled relatives of the land iguanas we'd encountered at the other end of the island.

"Are the two species closely related?" Heather asked.

"Yes," George replied. "The marine iguanas have adapted to grazing in the water. They feed on algae, sometimes as much as two hundred feet down."

"They're not indigenous, are they?" she went on.

"That depends on your definition. They evolved here from the land iguanas."

"What is the theory on how they got here?"

"Most people think they rode out on a log or some other form of vegetation."

"Come now. That's not a scientific explanation."

"Why not?" I asked. "And who cares, anyway?"

Heather gave me a withering look. I shrugged and moved off. I wanted to enjoy being in this incredible place, and their questions were driving me nuts. I felt sorry for George. He couldn't walk away.

Joe, Pat and I mingled with the sea lions. They seemed completely at ease with us. The older members of the group had sought out smooth rocky surfaces warmed by the sun. Others lolled in the sand near the water's edge. A young pair of twins played close to the adults. The rest of us—the older sea lions and the people—watched their games indulgently.

The sound of the outboard announced Hugo.

"It can't be time already." I was disappointed.

" 'Fraid so, Gwen," George said. "Peter runs a tight schedule."

3. En route to Barrington

Peter organized our lunch, then went topside to start the drive to Barrington. I was having a great time, but the others were not. We weren't fifteen minutes into the trip when it became clear they were seasick. I finished my lunch with George and joined the others on deck.

"Be sure you cover up," Peter reminded us. "Gwen, those shorts aren't going to do it."

"It's too hot for jeans. And you worry too much."

I sat in the cockpit, loving the feel of the wind as it rushed past. My hat provided shade for my face, and the dark glasses stopped the glare. Joe and Pat had found retreats up on the bow. They seemed to be feeling quietly queasy. It was David and Heather who were really sick. They sat on the cabin roof, backs to the sun, leaning heavily on one another. David was wearing the long-sleeved shirt, trousers, and chintz cap. He was barefoot. Heather, who tans well, wasn't as concerned about her face and arms, but she too wore long pants.

"David, put your socks back on," Peter ordered. "You're going to burn your feet."

"I can't stand to wear socks in this heat," David replied through clenched teeth.

"It wasn't a secret that you were going to hit the equatorial sun. Why didn't you bring clothes for it?"

David didn't respond.

"We believe in spontaneity," I said under the roar of the motor.

"That's all very well," Peter replied, also speaking softly. "But sometimes you have to be practical."

"This isn't about clothes, is it?"

"No. It's about Joe's bunk."

"He didn't make it up?"

"This is not a luxury cruise. We don't have time to make beds."

"I'd suggest you leave it unmade, but Joe would never notice. He lives like that at home, you know."

"I don't give a bloody damn what he does at home, but here he'd better have that bunk cleared off when it's time to eat."

"Fine. Tell him that, Peter."

"I will."

"Sure you will." George laughed.

I had a lovely afternoon. We were without benefit of questions, and conversation flowed easily among Peter, George and me.

When we neared Barrington, Hugo dropped a fishing line over the stern of the boat. I was amazed when he caught three enormous bonito in rapid succession. He cleaned them on the deck behind us. Two dozen or more frigate birds—huge, black creatures with bright red pouches and forked tails—gathered above us. Hugo tossed the fish heads and innards over the side, and the frigates dove frantically to catch the morsels before they hit the water.

"Look at them," I exclaimed. "Joe, Pat, come and see."

"Those birds are thieves," Peter said. "When other birds make a catch, the frigates will try to steal it right out of their beaks."

"Why don't they fish for themselves?"

"They can't. Their feathers have no protective oils. They'd become water-logged and drown. So their adaptation is to steal."

"I know some people like that."

"Hey, whatever works," Joe laughed.

4. Barrington

It was four when we dropped anchor in a beautiful secluded bay. George took us to a beautiful, sandy beach.

"We had planned to go swimming here," he commented, "but it's much too cold now. Once the sun is off the water, forget it."

He started off toward a trail. "Where are we going?" I asked.

"Up the hill to see the cactus."

"I'll stay here," Pat said. "There's a marvelous hawk over there. I want his picture."

"David, Heather, are you guys sure you want to walk?"

"You bet your sweet ass. We didn't come here to sit on the beach."

"I guess you don't want to hear that you look like hell."

He didn't answer. In silence, we hiked up a short, steep, path to a forest of giant cacti.

"As you can see, these trees have formed a much thicker protective coat than those on Plazas."

"These trunks look like yellow pines. We could be in the High Sierra."

"But look up. You won't find a crown of thick, green, spiky pads in your California mountains."

"George, what's the genus of these cacti?" Heather demanded.

I didn't want to hear this, so I turned back to the beach.

It was almost twilight. I joined Pat who was sitting on a log watching the hawk. When a second hawk arrived, the two of them glided back and forth, circling together and then flying apart.

We watched the moon come up behind the mating pair. The water and sky were deep blue with touches of crimson. The two regal birds were intent on their own magic. A star fell across the horizon, the sky winked from a million eyes, and, for a brief moment, I saw the lines of the world. We sat quietly, aware that these are, indeed, enchanted islands.

Our noisy friends broke the spell. Hugo picked us up and we returned to cocktail hour. Dinner was Hugo's specialty: ceviche— raw fish marinated in lemon juice with sliced onion—and fried tuna steaks.

"You really missed it, Pat," David said. "Those cacti have evolved into something unique— We are seeing evolution in real time."

"You missed an incredible experience right there on the beach," Pat said.

"You mean the hawks? You can see them any time. There are thousands of red tails back home. You're not going to make the most of this trip if you sit around watching birds."

Pat shook her head in annoyance. "Is there any more ceviche, Hugo?"

He beamed and served her another helping.

"Magnifico!" she exclaimed.

Over coffee, Peter reviewed the schedule for the next day. "It's a long drive to Hood. I'll be getting underway about two a.m. I want you to secure everything. That includes tying up the canvas 'halters' on the sides of your bunks. Pull them out from under the mattresses and secure them."

"That's ridiculous," Pat protested.

"Ridiculous it may be, but they must be in place tonight."

Grumbling, we set up our individual playpens and fell asleep.

The Bronzewing at rest off the cactus-strewn volcanic formation that is Plazas Island.

CHAPTER TWELVE
Barrington to Hood

1. Night travel

I heard Peter whisper "Hugo." Then the engine roared, the anchor clanged into place, and we were under way. I turned on my flashlight and peered at my watch. Four a.m. Thank God for Peter. The rocking motion of the boat lulled me back to sleep. I dozed until a shaft of light found its way through Peter's porthole, across the galley and into my eyes. The sunrise—

In my haste to escape from the bunk, I mistook Joe's shoulder for a footrest. He didn't stir. Emboldened, I grabbed my clothes and dressed beside his bunk. I had run the naked gauntlet undetected.

The coffee water was hot. I fixed a cup and joined Peter and Hugo in the cockpit. "What a gorgeous day. I was afraid I'd missed the sunrise."

"What you almost missed is the porpoises," Peter replied. "They're riding the pressure wave ahead of the bow. And some of them are racing us. Have a look over there!"

Three dorsal fins streaked, in close formation, through the waves. Then the dolphins shot out of the water in a perfect arc. A second trio lifted into the air nearby.

I made my way to the bow and sat with my legs hanging over the sides. The wave riders were so close I could almost touch them with my feet.

2. Some of us get seasick

I was still on the bow when Joe appeared an hour later. "Come look at the dolphins," I yelled. "They might cheer you up."

He ignored me. I joined him in the cockpit just as David and Heather crawled out.

"I gather it's not great sleeping up front," I said. "You're both green."

"I don't want to talk about it," Heather replied.

They climbed onto the cabin roof and huddled together.

"Don't you want to see the dolphins?"

"No. You should go help Pat. We couldn't manage."

I found Pat leaning over her bunk, struggling with the sheets. "What's wrong?"

"I can't get the bed made. Every time I start to pull the covers up, the boat rolls and I get seasick again."

I reached out to take the sheets from her, but she fell on top of them. "You are in bad shape. Go on up. I'll finish this."

She disappeared without a word.

I finished making her bunk and stowed her gear out of the way. When I returned to the deck, Peter asked if the coast was clear for breakfast. Since we would be sitting on Pat's bunk to eat, that was relevant. I told him all was well, and he sent Hugo off to cook. I was in my element, chatting with George and Peter while the others tried to find holes to crawl into. I wasn't very sympathetic. It was so wonderful to be able to talk without being interrupted constantly. I was in a great mood when Peter said that breakfast was ready. This announcement was received with silence.

"You guys aren't coming?" I asked. "Toast? Coffee?" Again no answer. "We'll miss you," I said, going below.

George, Hugo and I ate in silence. Then Peter came down while George navigated.

"The good news is it'll be quiet today," I said to Peter. "You must be bored to death with Heather's questions."

"Not really. Most tourists are like that. Especially Americans."

"Heather's English. I should think you would have noticed."

"She's as American as you are. She'd have to take a refresher course in reticence to get through customs back home. But you surprise me. Don't you think curiosity's healthy?"

"Not when it stops the experience. Not when you miss the beauty."

"They must be seeing it. They're always taking pictures."

"With them, seeing's O.K., feeling isn't. Which is their business as long as they don't interfere with me. But the trouble is, they do. The jabbering drives me crazy."

"You need ear plugs, love."

"You think I can just turn them off?"

"No, we all have our flash points. Joe is the one who gets to me. He expects to be waited on. We don't have time to make his bed."

"Peter, I told you. Joe doesn't know what a made bed looks like. It's not personal."

"It feels personal."

"I'll talk to him when he's healthier."

"Speaking of which, we'd better go check on sickbay."

The patients were scattered around the deck, seeking privacy where there was none.

"I hope you're all using suntan lotion," Peter said loudly. "Hood is seventy kilometers from Barrington, and we're fighting the currents. We can't provide shade. You'll fry if you stay topside."

"David, maybe you should go below," I said.

"Are you out of your mind?" He was standing on the steps, his arms resting on either side of the cabin roof. Heather's bonnet was providing scant relief from the sun. He looked hot and ill. "I have it figured out. If you let your stomach move with the boat instead of trying to hold it steady, it's not so bad."

"You're really into control, aren't you?" I laughed. He didn't reply.

3. Gardiner Bay

I enjoyed having time alone with Peter and George. We spotted several albatrosses and a number of frigate birds, but little else. It was three when Peter dropped anchor in Gardiner Bay on Hood Island.

The others revived when the motion stopped.

"What, still alive?" I chided David.

"Yes, and I heard every word you said."

"That's bad news."

"The swimming is good here," Peter said. "Cold, but nice."

"Gwen, are you putting on your bathing suit?" Heather asked.

"No. I'm taking off my clothes. Fancy underwear will have to do."

"Well—" She looked daggers at me. "David, where are you going?"

"What does it look like? I'm too damned hot." He jumped into the water and swam ashore.

The rest of us waited for the dinghy and walked into the surf from the beach. We swam with a group of sea lions, then put our towels down between two harems. They accepted our presence without complaint. When I ventured too close to one of the babies, a young bull made threatening gestures and lunged at me until I moved away. Full of himself, he approached an older bull, and was thoroughly routed.

"What are you staring at, David?" I asked.

"That's quite a bathing suit."

"The price is right. It's underwear."

"It looks great. Heather, why don't you—"

"You surely don't think I'd appear in public in my underwear. David, where's my camera? I want to photograph the sea lions."

I started to respond, but George interrupted. "Anyone for a walk down the beach?"

Joe was asleep. Pat walked with us for a while, then stopped to photograph the rock formation offshore. George and I didn't wait.

"Look at these tunnel-worm nests," he said. "They're made of sand and, well, tunnel-worm glue. There are hundreds of tiny, intricate chambers—"

"—and   all the sand colors—white, green, red, yellow—We only have white sand in California."

"It's different in volcano land."

"The islands are fascinating. You're lucky to be staying long enough to really see them."

"Two years is a bit much. It's all starting to look the same."

"Why the Galapagos? Why not Canada?"

"Hindsight says Canada would have been a better choice. But I thought I'd learn Spanish here, see a bit of the world."

"And you did," I pointed out.

"Not really. I didn't learn Spanish. I'm stuck here on the islands, and I don't belong."

"How so?"

"I'm not a scientist. They put me through their guide training program at the Darwin Station, but I don't know enough to help those guys."

"You haven't made friends?"

"Not really. Everyone's busy— I get so damned homesick— It's awful, knowing you can't go home."

"You can't get into the country?"

"No, and there's more. My father's written me off, my mother's heart is broken, and my girlfriend's engaged to a Marine. Sometimes I wish I'd gone to Nam and gotten myself killed—" He turned to look out at the ocean.

He seemed lost in thought. I waited for a while, then reached out and touched his arm. "I'm sorry, George. It probably doesn't help, but I think you were right not to go."

He smiled at me. "Thanks. I'm O.K. Really. It'll be over soon, and meanwhile I'm working with groups like yours—"

"You can't mean you've had numerous other groups like ours, George."

"You're right. This is a first." He glanced at his watch. "It's five-thirty. We'd better turn back."

We dined in splendor: Hugo and Peter had found lobster. We had the traditional rum and grapefruit juice cocktails, ceviche appetizers, and lobster entree, and then sat on deck, hypnotized by the near-full moon and the brilliant stars. We watched in silence as an owl flew down to perch on the mast. His outline was sharp against the night sky—an awesome, welcoming presence.

4. Exploring Hood

"This one's for Gwen," Peter announced. "Today we show off the Bronzewing. No motors allowed."

She caught the wind in her sail and heeled over, slipping through the swells with fish-like ease. I was thrilled. This was what I'd expected, sailing the seas in the Galapagos Islands. We had a splendid run around the end of the island to Puenta Suarez, and I was beside myself with joy.

David, on the other hand, was miserable. His insistence on exposing his bare feet to the sun the day before had resulted in a horrendous case of sunburn. Gamely, he prepared for what George had described as a wet landing.

Hugo dumped us offshore and we waded, barefoot, through a throng of noisy sea lions. This must have been a favored birthing spot. We passed many tiny babies, one with his cord still attached. He was guarded by his mother and an aggressive bull.

"I'll be damned," Pat said."The placenta's on that rock, and the finches are eating it."

"So?"

"These finches are supposed to be vegetarians."

"She's right," Heather said. "Why are they doing that, George?"

"I guess they're hungry. Don't forget, the National Park rule says you must stay on the trail."

We hadn't walked a hundred feet when we came upon nesting blue-footed boobies in our path. "What in hell are they doing?" I asked.

"The trail was supposed to give the boobies privacy for nesting. But the birds liked the cleared path, and built their nests on it. So we get to walk right through the nursery."

"The blue-foots look like the, uh, other boobies. The masked ones," Joe said.

"How so?" George asked. "They have no masks and their feet are blue. Or do you mean the insane look in the eyes?"

"It's more than a look," Pat said. "These nests are proof of insanity."

Some of the blue-foots were holding their eggs between large, blue-veined incubators. Some perched above tiny chicks whose curious heads poked out from under fur-like feathers. One pair was arguing with a hungry, fluffed-out chick tall enough to look them in the eye.

"Now we're coming into masked booby territory," George said.

"They're all over. I can't move without stepping on one," Joe laughed.

"Do all boobies nest on flat, clear areas?" Heather asked.

"No. Wait until you see the red-foots. They build nests a few feet off the ground, on the tops of low-growing shrubs. These are all adaptations to the space problems here in the Galapagos."

"We'll miss the red-foots," Heather said. "We aren't going to Tower."

"It was that or miss the waved albatrosses here on Hood," Pat said. "We are seeing a lot of booby birds."

"I suppose you're right," Heather agreed. "And where exactly are the albatrosses?"

"On top of the plateau."

The sun was blistering. George led us to a shady spot under high volcanic rocks. While we rested, we watched a horde of brightly colored marine iguanas.

"George, I thought marine iguanas were black," Heather said.

"You can't generalize from island to island. These are typical of what you'll find on Hood. Look how their skins gleam against the black lava."

"This is a great spot for pictures." Pat was mounting her zoom lens on the body of her Nikon. "I can see fur seals, lava lizards, mockingbirds, finches, boobies— And there's an oyster catcher."

"Good," I replied. "You can stay here while we hike up to see the albatrosses."

"I don't want to miss them."

"But Pat, it's a climb—"

"You go on ahead. I'll take my time."

"At least let me carry your camera."

We were halfway up the trail when David said, "I'm going to take a break."

"Are your feet O.K.?" George asked.

"Not especially. You guys go on."

5. Albatrosses

George, Joe and I climbed quickly to the plateau. "This is the albatross nesting area. When they finally leave for the open sea, they stay a long time. Some say as long as seven years."

"I saw one sleeping on the water this morning," I said. "When he woke up, he ran on the surface and flapped his wings. It took him several tries to get airborne."

"They're more awkward than that on land."

"How so?"

"They live on the water—eating and sleeping—for so long, they seem to forget how hard land is. When they come back here to mate, they sometimes break a wing or a leg during the landing."

"They remember this place all that time?"

"Yes. As you can see, the young are raised here. This seems to be their sacred place. I wouldn't bring a large group anywhere near here. But you guys are careful. I'm going to let you wander around a little."

We walked slowly through the nesting birds, enjoying their awkwardness. Some of the chicks were almost fledged. They looked foolish, with feathers on their bodies, but caps of down on their heads. They were screaming angrily at the adults for food.

We were delighted to find a pair doing the sky-pointing mating ritual. The two birds faced each other, as if doing a menuet, honking, moving from side to side, and raising their beaks rhythmically toward the sun. To our amazement, a third bird, evidently learning the routine, joined them at one side and proceeded to imitate each in turn.

"Is that how they learn the mating ritual?" I asked George.

He shrugged. "Guess so."

Pat caught up with us and I handed her the camera.

"Just look at them, Pat," I said excitedly.

"I know," she replied. "This is why I had to come."

"You were right."

We watched for almost an hour, then moved on to what appeared to be flight school. Adult birds use the flat area at the top of the plateau to get up speed before hurling themselves off the cliff and into the wind currents. Chicks were practicing take-off procedures, flapping their wings ferociously and making little running starts toward the edge. The older ones ran farther, always putting on the brakes at the last minute.

"It's time for lunch," George said.

"You can't mean it," I said. "This is incredible."

"We can come back here this afternoon if you like."

"And again the next day and the next … "

6. More albatrosses

It was two-thirty when Hugo ferried us back to shore.

"Why didn't David come?" Joe asked as we started up the trail.

"His feet are a mess," Heather replied. "He has blisters the size of quarters on the soles. He almost didn't make it down the trail this morning."

"That sounds dreadful," Pat said.

"Thank heaven for you, Pat. I need help with my camera. David always takes the pictures for me."

"I'll be too far behind to help."

"I'll walk with you. We can stop whenever you see something of interest. Like those boobies on their nest. How should I stand? The sun's almost overhead, but they're in the shade—"

"We'll leave you to it," George said. "Everybody's headed for the albatrosses, right? Joe, Gwen, let's go."

"Why are you laughing, Joe?" I asked as we moved on.

"Pat's going to be pretty upset by dinner time."

"She'll need an extra drink," George commented.

At the top of the plateau, we sat down on a log near the albatross runway. The youngest birds mimicked their older friends, making little false starts, flapping inadequate wings, wobbling on unsure feet. The older, nearly-fledged birds were racing down the ramp toward the cliff, flapping wings outspread, eyes fixed on the horizon. Each attempt brought them a few inches closer to the edge, and we held our breaths in anticipation of one of them taking that giant leap into the future. But our mood, and possibly theirs, was broken when Heather and Pat caught up.

"George, what's the wing span on the adults?"

"I don't know. They're big—maybe nine feet?"

"That's more the size of a condor, isn't it?" Pat asked. "I think an albatross is more like eight feet."

"I'd like to know. Who has the bird book?"

"It's back at the boat."

"What a nuisance. David always brings the bird book. None of these has a span of more than six feet."

"Seven," Joe said. "I'm sure that one coming now has at least seven feet of wing. Look at him. He's going to— Damn, he braked again."

On our way back, we stopped at the blow hole. Each ocean swell sent a geyser high into the air. Standing fifteen feet away, we were enveloped by a fine mist. Up close, we would have been drenched. George handed bananas around. Darwin finches joined us to fight over the peels.

We were almost down the trail when we came upon a fledgling albatross, looking like a gawky teenager as he attempted to join a group of boobies. They were not welcoming him.

"George, what is he doing here?" Heather asked.

"I haven't the vaguest notion."

"He looks so silly," Pat said. "Wait. I have to get a picture of this."

7. An evening out of time

It was after five when we returned to the Bronzewing. David was much improved, and very interested in our explorations. "Heather, did you get pictures?"

"Yes, and Pat showed me how to keep the reflection of the sun off the lens. It's quite simple, really, you just—"

They disappeared into the cabin and we collapsed in the cockpit. We sat over drinks, enjoying the warm, soft evening breeze. Sunset faded to gray light, and the moon appeared. Layers of clouds in her path created the effect of multiple moon rises. Finally she emerged, full, to cast light on the bay, light that melted into the gentle swells of the ocean.

It was an evening out of time. There were no questions over dinner, only good conversation. When we moved to the back of the boat, George brought out his guitar and serenaded us with songs from the sixties. We sang along with him. His music evoked an unheard of camaraderie. We lingered over it like rare brandy.

Albatross training in flight school on Hood Island.

CHAPTER THIRTEEN
Academy Bay, Santa Cruz

1. Civilization intrudes

Our explorations were interrupted by a supply stop in Academy Bay. This sprawling Ecuadorian fishing village nestles in the soft curve on the lee side of Santa Cruz. As the principal gringo colony in the Galapagos, it is also the usual resting place for tourists.

Hugo pulled the dinghy around.

"It's a waste of time to spend two days ashore," Heather said. "We want to be out seeing the other islands."

"Too bad about that, love," Peter replied. "It'll take me two days to round up what we need for the rest of the trip. Besides, you people need a chance to clean up."

"One day should be adequate," Heather insisted.

"I'm talking gas and bread. Come on, love, be reasonable."

David and Heather groused all the way to the dock. We had arrived at the only hotel, a modest, one-story affair on the water. Hugo lugged our bags into the lobby and Peter checked us in. We spent an hour cleaning up, then regrouped in the lobby. Peter had told us laundry service was included with the room, so we had gathered up all our clothes. We dumped them in front of the desk, creating a small mountain of rags.

"They may have to change their rules." Peter laughed when he saw the mess. "O.K., everybody, into the jeep. We're going for a tour of the island."

On the outskirts of town, we entered farm country: small houses, spreading green trees, and lush crops surrounded each settlement.

"Get a load of those funny shaped hedges," Joe said.

"Those aren't hedges," George replied. "They're living fences. The wood comes from a tree that regenerates. The cuttings root and continue to grow."

"Like I said, you get funny shaped hedges."

"I'll tell you what's strange. After a while, you get so used to seeing new growth on fences that you do a double take when you come across a dead one. I was in Guayaquil last month, and I said to my friend, 'What's wrong with that fence?'"

"A little shift in reality is good for the digestion," David said. "Hey, the country road just turned into a super highway. What's that about?"

"It's about the beginning of the end," Peter shouted over his shoulder. "This road will bisect the island and connect with a boat service to Baltra. We're talking tourism with a capital T."

Pat leaned forward so that Peter could hear her. "This place is too fragile for vast numbers of tourists. They'll love it to death."

"But Ecuador needs the money. And tourism is a convincing argument for protecting wildlife."

"I hate it when everything beautiful is hanging by a thread," I said.

We drove on in silence, as if imagining the engine noise that had allowed us easy personal distance in the plane. We drove up and up, through the rural foothills. I watched in wonder as the landscape transitioned into a tropical paradise. And then we topped the crest of the mountain.

Peter slowed to a crawl. "Baltra's straight ahead. You'll see it from this turnout."

"Maybe we can spot the plane," Joe said.

David stood up and grabbed his binoculars. "I'd like that a lot."

Peter had stopped at road's end. An enormous pile of construction materials lay nearby. We climbed up a steep sand pile for a better look.

"I can't see the plane," Joe said.

"Try these, Joe." Peter handed over his binoculars.

"I still can't make her out. Damn! The landing strip is clear enough, but it's empty."

"The plane must be obscured by a tree, don't you think?" Heather asked. "Or a building?"

"There weren't any trees near the runway," I said.

"The buildings were at the far end," Joe added. "Here, let me have another look."

Despite our efforts, no one caught as much as a glimpse of our two-winged friend. I was secretly delighted to think our plane might have been hot-wired. That would mean returning to the mainland on the charter flight, and, if my luck held, taking a commercial flight home. But the others were worried, and I tried to sound supportive as we headed toward Academy Bay.

It was dusk. Peter spotted an owl on a fence post and pulled over.

"David, where's the camera—"

"I want that shot," Joe said. "Pat, aren't you getting him?"

"The light's terrible, but it's worth a try."

I wandered off for a moment of silence in the eerie twilight.

2. Dinner on the town

Pat was tired. She skipped dinner and went to bed. Heather and David ate at the hotel. But Joe and I wanted to taste our freedom. We wandered into town and joined the locals at the only restaurant. It also served as a bar and general purpose hangout. No one spoke English, but we managed to order beer and fried fish. The beer was served instantly.

"Do you suppose it's endemic?" I asked.

"What? The beer?" He laughed. "Heather and David don't do that back home."

"Everything changes when you're confined with people. And there's no escaping them on the Bronzewing."

"Ah yes, the Bronzewing." Joe raised his glass in salute.

"You don't like her?"

"She's been fine. I haven't. Being seasick is not my idea of fun. I'm enjoying being on solid ground."

We had planned to walk after dinner, but decided against it. We were so sleepy, it took all our energy to find the hotel.

Our three long, skinny beds, were lined up against the wall, dormitory style. I fell into the middle one and pulled off my jeans and T-shirt. I missed the rocking of the boat, but slipped easily into a deep sleep. I have no idea how much time had passed, but the lights were out when an enormous crash jarred me awake.

"What the hell was that?" Pat asked.

"Goddamnbedfelldownonme." Joe's voice was muffled.

"Wait a minute. Where's the light?" I yelled.

"I've got it," Pat replied. "Thank heaven the generator's still going." The dim bulb cast a blurred glow on a billowing mass of blankets and pillows intertwined with the corners of a mattress. Only Joe's head was visible.

Pat and I burst out laughing. "Good trick, Joe," I said, pulling my jeans back on.

"You're supposed to be outside the bed when you fold it up," Pat said. "How did you manage this?"

"Will you can the sarcasm? Get me out of here!"

We pulled him free and then discovered that his bed slats had been improperly installed. He had fallen through them to the floor. We remade the bed frame, then the bed, and stashed him in it.

"Comfy?" I asked.

"Sure. I'm just great. If the ocean doesn't get you, the bed slats will."

"Sleep carefully, Joe. I don't want any more shocks tonight."

I thought I'd go right back to sleep, but I couldn't stop giggling.

"And exactly what is so funny?" Joe asked.

"I keep remembering how silly you looked, all tangled up in that bed."

"Would you like to try it? I'd be happy to show you how it works. Or you could just shut up."

"What a good idea. Sleep well."

3. A quiet day

In the morning, we joined Heather and David in the tiny dining room.

"Good grief, David," I said. "Where did you get that gorgeous shirt?"

"It ought to look familiar," he replied. "It's the one you bought in Guayaquil."

"I can't make the toaster work," Joe said.

"That was white," I said. "This one has orange tubes down to the wrists."

"Heather did that last night," David said.

"I bought the material here in the village," Heather told us.

"The generator doesn't come on until seven," Pat said.

"Isn't this great? Now I have a long-sleeved shirt."

"I would have sworn you were wearing a giant orange worm under your shirt."

"Compliments, compliments. Tell me, Gwen, will it do for our farewell dinner?"

"Farewell dinner?"

"We have lights," Pat announced. "The generator's on."

"Yes. In Acapulco. We thought we'd go back to the Hyatt Regency. What do you think?"

"Joe, try the toaster again."

"You'll be a knockout."

"I hope they serve quickly," Heather said. "George will be here soon."

"You're going up the mountain today?" I asked.

"We all are," she replied.

Pat stood up. "I'm going back to sleep."

"I think I'll pass," I said. "I want to catch up on my writing."

"You do that all the time. This is our only chance to see the Tortoise Preserve. There are several Galapagos species—"

"I'm just not in the mood, O.K.?"

George was surprised that I wasn't joining them. "It's a very special place."

"I can't handle too many special places at one time. Go. Have fun. I'll see you later." I waved goodbye and set off on my walk.

My path took me past the generator. The water cycled through the system and into the community laundry. Tubs had been provided, and several women were already at work. I met others en route, carrying the day's washing in large baskets.

And then, in what seemed an instant, I was alone in nowhere. As I walked on, I felt a surge of energy, a connection with the urgent forces of life all around me. Perhaps it was the enchantment Pat had spoken of. I had not felt it before. And now it flowed through my body, bringing sharpened awareness. I sat down on a rock and watched the underbrush. Two colorful lizards returned my gaze. They seemed like messengers and I sat with them a long time.

When I moved, it was like breaking a spell. It had been a magical experience, yet almost too much to deal with. I started back, feeling lightheaded. As I passed the generator, the enchantment disappeared. It was still laundry day, the sun was shining, the women were gossiping over their work. It had, perhaps, been a dream.

I read much of the day. It was after two when Peter stopped by to check on Pat.

"Your laundry's on the line. Did you see it?"

"No. I suppose Heather's white longies are there?"

"The whole bit. You can't miss it. It's right by the main road." He paused. "How come you didn't go with the others?"

"I needed a day off. It's quiet here. I'm having a great time."

"But you're missing one of the best things on the trip—"

"I'm fine. Don't worry about it. How's the resupply effort going?"

"I'm getting the usual. Ecuadorian time is different. The baker told me this morning the bread would be ready at noon. At noon, he told me three o'clock. I'll try again in an hour. You either learn to slow down or die of aggravation."

Over dinner we heard tales of mating giant tortoises scraping shells like boulders in an avalanche. "You really missed it, Gwen," David said.

"I had a pretty nice day, myself. I think it may be hard to have a bad experience here."

"Pat, how's your film supply?" David reached across the table for a third slice of bread. "We used too much today."

"I just brought enough for myself. Don't they sell film in the village?"

"You would not believe what they charge. I bought two rolls, but it's ridiculous."

"They must have film at the Darwin Station," Heather suggested.

"Peter said they wouldn't part with any. Tourists always run out of film."

"If only we could do something for them—like take some photos from the air."

"We can." Joe looked pleased with himself. "We have enough extra gas to do a flyover before we leave."

"That's it, then," Heather said. "We'll photograph the centers of the volcanos. They'll die for pictures like that."

4. Santa Cruz society

Peter collected us early in the morning for our visit to the Darwin Station. "This is a major research center," he told us. "It was started by UNESCO, the World Wildlife Fund and many other organizations. People come here from everywhere to do research."

We met several of the visiting scientists and more of the resident tortoises, and heard about the various cooperative breeding programs that will, with luck, ensure the existence of the remarkably diverse giant tortoises. David took each of the scientists aside to make his plea for film. He came away with five rolls. His aggressiveness was embarrassing but effective.

After lunch we were scheduled to visit the local gringo colony. I was pleased at the prospect of meeting some new people. Living in such cramped quarters with these relative strangers had been a strain. Just for starters, the number of separate relationships in our group was the combination of five objects taken two at a time. The addition of Peter, George and Hugo had diluted the tension. A few more people could only improve the situation.

Peter brought the dinghy to the hotel dock, and we hopped in for our trip to the "Residential" section of Academy Bay.

I was trailing my hand in the water, enjoying the cool feel, when David said, "So we got rid of George. Isn't that great?"

I was stunned. "What in hell are you talking about?"

"Tui de Roy has agreed to be our guide. Now we can really find out what's what on the islands. She'll know which animals are indigenous."

"You fired George?"

"We'd heard everything he had to say. We told Peter how we all felt, and he fired him."

My response was cut short by our arrival at the marine iguana capital of the world. This was a house built of huge slabs of rock at the corner of the bay, a house inhabited by hundreds of marine iguanas and one remarkable man. Carl Angemeyer, handsome, tanned, about sixty, was dressed casually for the filming of a documentary. Japanese filmmakers were swarming like the iguanas.

Carl accepted our arrival with nonchalance. Visitors were an every day occurrence. He ordered up rice and shrimp for his friends (the iguanas, not us), and stood chatting (with us, not the iguanas). The dark, crested creatures were everywhere: the roof, the patio, the driveway. They climbed through the paneless windows and down the walls to reach their treat. When they encountered friends, they paused and nodded, much as the Japanese film crew had done.

It was a fascinating environment, but I had trouble appreciating it. My mind was full of questions about George and Tui. I could feel my unexpressed anger searching for a way out and opting for a tension headache.

Peter was stiff and formal as he escorted us on the short beach-front walk to the home of Mrs. Seavers. I followed slowly, my hands clasped behind my back. As I walked, I stared down at the trail, trying vainly to stop the pain by keeping my head still.

A shrub-lined path led to the veranda. White wicker tables were already set. Mrs. Seavers greeted us. A reserved, heavy-set, middle-aged woman, she told us she and her husband had come from Germany several years before.

The coffee, grown on Santa Cruz, was rich, almost like espresso. I thought I might feel better if I ate something. The cakes and cookies, worthy of the finest German bakery, were a mistake. I concentrated on the tame finches who were finishing the crumbs on saucers. They cavorted around the table, as if participating in the conversation.

We were all startled when a stunning young woman burst through the hedge and hurried up the path.

"Tui," Mrs. Seavers said. "Come and meet the guests. This is Tui de Roy."

"You're going to be our guide for the rest of our trip." Heather held out her hand. "Thank you for agreeing to come with us."

"It couldn't be better for me," Tui replied. "I haven't been out to the other islands for a couple of months and I miss them."

"Tui, dear, did you bring some of your jewelry to show the guests? Tui and her family make these necklaces and earrings from local shells and rocks. And I think she has some of her photos, as well."

"You don't have much opportunity to market these things, do you?" Heather asked.

"It used to be easy. Yachts would stop to resupply and we'd meet the people. But now that the Galapagos is a National Park, they are avoiding us."

"That's a shame," David said.

"You have to think of the wildlife first," she answered.

I stared at a print of tiny Galapagos tortoises. I liked it. And I liked the earrings. But I felt terrible and talking seemed like a bad idea. I was worried about George. Being fired wouldn't help his state of mind.

"Here comes Gil. This is my younger brother."

"Have some cookies, dear," Mrs. Seavers said.

A good looking young man, Gil seemed shy. But David

asked about the family boat project, and soon he was deep into an animated discussion. Part of me wanted to listen, the other part wanted to scream.

5. I have it out with Heather

Peter returned, and the rest of the group went with Gil to see the boat. I didn't need any more diversions. I followed Peter toward the next stop. Finally, I broke the silence.

"I guess you know I'm not exactly thrilled that you fired George."

Peter stopped and turned to face me. "You mean you didn't want to get rid of him? They told me—"

"Of course not. He's a decent, hard-working—"

"But David and Heather said you were as fed up with him as they were. And they told me you refused to go on the hike yesterday because of him. That's what really convinced me."

For a moment I was speechless. "You mean they— I didn't go because of them. They are driving me nuts in case you hadn't noticed." I took a deep breath. "George may not be the most knowledgeable guy in the world, but he has cooked our meals, guided us about, tried to answer our endless questions, fixed our drinks— What the hell do they want for a lousy ten bucks a day? Sure Tui's the expert on the islands. That doesn't warrant dumping George."

"I should have known."

Unable to think of anything else to say, we walked on to Gus' cave. Peter had told us about Carl's brother, Gus. Over the years, this eccentric bachelor had used lava and concrete to construct an irregular building that resembled a cave. Or so Peter had told us. From the outside, it looked like a rather large mud hut.

I paused at the entrance. "Why have you brought me here?"

"Everyone comes here. It's part of the standard tour. Gus's collection of bones, rocks, driftwood—it's all part of the Galapagos ambience."

"I've had quite enough ambience for one day— "

"Welcome to Gus' cave." The voice was deep and resonant. I turned to see a bearded figure in the doorway. He beckoned us in. "Hello, Peter."

"Good to see you, Gus. This is Gwen Moore, one of the tourists on the Bronzewing. The others are on their way."

In the dim light, I could barely make out the wizened face. He was eyeing me intently. He took my hand in both of his. "And where is your nest, Gwen?"

"Nest? Why, er, in Los Angeles."

"And you've come all this way to see Gus' enchanted junk." He nodded vigorously, like one of Carl's iguanas. I found myself mimicking the greeting. "Come, let me show you. These are my sculptures of the dance of life."

"Driftwood is beautiful, isn't it?"

"Not driftwood, my dear. Sculptures. Look closely. You can see all of life reflected here—birth, death, joy, sorrow, disease, male, female, copulation."

"It's marvelous, Gus. You must have spent years finding these things. Like that huge bone—"

"A jaw bone. Yes, the jaw bone of a whale."

I tried to listen, but the whole scene struck me as absurd.

I had to bite my tongue to keep from laughing. It was a relief when the others arrived. I moved away and found a place to sit, surrounded by the collection. Viewed from the inside, this was, indeed, a cave. The walls sloped up to meet in a crooked line, and portions of the floor were raised a few inches. The clutter covered every accessible surface. The room was lighted with candles and a fire, creating an effective change of mood in the growing darkness. Gus was a natural actor. In dramatic whispers, he told the newcomers the secrets of his vast collection of enchanted junk.

His intense feeling for the beauty of nature, in all its various stages of decay, was obvious. Suddenly, the clutter was clutter no longer. It had a pattern and a meaning that triumphed over the superficial phoniness of the cave and its creator. I felt his love and his pain.

But I couldn't stand to feel anything more. My anger was swallowing me up. I had to deal with it. Now. I crossed the room and spoke to Heather.

"I must talk to you. Outside."

She followed me to Gus' enchanted outdoor dump. "How dare you? That was a God damned bitchy thing to do, using me to get George fired."

"You didn't want him fired? But we have Tui, and she's—"

"I know all about Tui. You had a chance to hire her in the first place but no. You didn't want to spend all that money on a guide. Then it turns out we must have a guide, and George isn't up to your standards, so you dump him."

"George isn't my problem—"

"Being human isn't your problem, either. You've got your feelings so bottled up you wouldn't know where to look for them."

"I must have misunderstood. When you didn't go on the hike, we assumed you were as tired of George's banalities as we were—"

"You could have asked."

"I suppose you're right. Well, there's not much we can do about it now, is there? I am sorry, I really did misunderstand."

"You're right. There's nothing to be done. In the future, check things out, will you? I have a right to speak for myself."

"You do that very well."

I laughed, but it didn't help. Getting it said hadn't helped. I still felt like hell.

We rejoined the group. They were sitting on the floor on bits and pieces of animal fur, listening to a wobbly rendition of the Moonlight Sonata. The feeble Beethoven, the flickering candlelight, created a remarkable gestalt. I didn't want to miss it. But my attempt to go with the mood made my head throb.

6. A sad farewell

When we finally took our leave, I thought we were returning to the boat. But Peter had scheduled dinner at Mrs. Seavers'. The thought of eating was too much. I was relieved when the dear lady showed me to a back room and encouraged me to lie down with a cold cloth over my eyes. I slept until it was time to leave.

The moonless sky was dark when Peter drove us back to the boat. He let us off, then turned the dinghy around and headed back to shore. He was going after Hugo who was apparently out on the town. Pat and Joe went off to bed. I moved to the forward deck and collapsed against the mast. David found me there.

"Heather told me you were upset."

"Furious, to be exact."

"I'm sorry. I guess we were in the wrong that time."

"If you want to know what I think, ask."

Heather's voice startled me. "So we've done that now. Enough's been said on the subject, don't you agree?"

"No," David replied. "If we're going to learn anything from this, we have to talk about it."

We were interrupted by the arrival of an oar-driven dinghy. We stared into the darkness. Suddenly a form appeared over the side.

"Hi." It was Tui. "I'm leaving my gear." She tossed some bundles on the deck and started back over the side. "And there's a bundle from the hotel. I think it's laundry."

I giggled. "That has to be Joe's. He never remembers to pack his clothes."

"Where's she going?" Heather asked.

"How should I know?"

Moments later, an outboard announced another boat. I assumed it was Peter returning, and was pleasantly surprised when George appeared.

We moved to the cockpit to greet him.

"I came after my belongings," he said. "And to say goodbye."

"There's something you should know, George," David said. "Pat and Gwen did not have any complaints about your work. I apologize for misstating the situation."

"It's O.K. I told you in the first place that Tui knew a lot more than I do. And she's not depressed."

"Hey, that's not your fault—" I said.

"Yes, actually, it is. So, how about one farewell song?"

George took out his guitar and played a sad, lonely, country western tune. We were still hearing it when he slipped back into the night.

CHAPTER FOURTEEN
Academy Bay to Tortuga Island and Villamil

1. I talk to Tui

I awoke to a painful throbbing. My head— No, it was the roar of the engine. The headache still burned, but it was ninety-five percent contained. Relieved, I got up slowly, and added two aspirin to the morning ritual. Tui and Peter were talking quietly in the cockpit.

"Good morning." Peter raised his hand in salute. "How are you?"

"Better, thanks. Nothing like a little sleep. You might try it sometime."

"What do you mean? I slept until three."

"That long! What about you, Tui? Did he get you up?"

"Only long enough to grab my sleeping bag and move down to his bunk. The deck's all very well until the boat starts moving. I had a great sleep."

"And it's high time you earned your keep," Peter said. "Here, take the tiller for a while."

"You're going back to bed?"

"I'm going to speak to Hugo. Now that you're here, he'll have to stop singing dirty songs in Spanish."

Tui laughed and took his seat. She pushed the stray strands of blond hair under her kerchief and pointed at a nearby land mass. "That's Isabella. It's the largest of the islands. We'll be going all the way around her." She looked away from me. "Peter told me you were upset about George. I'm sorry it was handled so badly. I'll talk to him when I get back."

"Thanks. He seemed pretty down."

"It's hard for me to imagine, being down in this place."

"I would agree, but I've been going through a pretty lengthy depression myself."

"Really? You don't look it."

"Now that you mention it, I don't feel it."

"Why were you depressed?"

"I'm not sure. And I'm probably better off not remembering. It'll catch up with me soon enough. I want you to know I'm glad you're here. I don't like what happened to George, but that's a separate issue. Heather should have hired you in the first place."

"When she called me in Berkeley?"

I nodded.

"I told her I was available. She said you didn't need a guide."

"She didn't want to spend the money."

"She can't be that poor."

"Hell no. She's a successful scientist. But David, he's her lover in case you hadn't noticed—"

"I wondered. They aren't very demonstrative."

"They show affection by fussing over each other. 'David, you forgot your hat.' 'Here, Heather, I'll take the picture.' David's struggling financially, and she's protecting his fragile male ego. Which, according to me, doesn't need help."

"So if she didn't want to hire me as a guide, why bother to call me in the first place?"

"To check out the itinerary. She's very impressed with you."

Tui smiled. "I thought she had me mixed up with someone else. Here I was on my first trip out of the islands, and she asked if I was bored."

"That was your first trip?"

"Aside from leaving Belgium when I was two, yes. It was quite a challenge, traveling on my own. Especially New York. The Audubon people couldn't meet my plane, and I had to find my way on the subway."

"Coffee?" Peter asked. We both nodded and he disappeared into the cabin.

"How did you manage the subway?"

"I've spent my whole life in wilderness. The New York subway's more of the same."

"New Yorkers don't handle your world as well as you handle theirs."

"I'd say our navigational skills are about equal. They do fine down here in yachts."

"But you'd be O.K. anywhere in the world. That comes from living with nature."

"You may be right. Nature makes you deal with the person you really are. You can't pretend. Oh, good. We're coming to Tortuga, that island over there with the steep sides."

"Are there a lot of turtles on Tortuga?"

"Not one. The name comes from the way the crescent rises in the middle. It's the silhouette of the high-domed Galapagos tortoise."

"Can we go in a little closer?"

"Sure," Tui replied, pulling the tiller toward her.

2. The frigate birds

Peter was handing us coffee when Heather and David emerged.

"David, you found a hat!" I stood up for a better look. "A Panama hat, at that."

"It's the only one I could find in the village."

"The bonnet had more style."

"You really know how to hurt a guy. Tui, did you say that's Tortuga? Are we seeing the end of a large island?"

"You're seeing all of it. It's the rim of a submerged volcano."

We rounded the end of the crescent and headed up the concave side of the islet. The slope was covered with hundreds of frigate birds.

"Is that all one species?" Heather asked.

"No, there are two—the Great and the Magnificent. The birds aren't large, but they're impressive with their glossy black coats and long, forked tails."

"They seem to be everywhere in the Galapagos," Heather said. "How big are the wings?"

"About seven feet. They use that span to glide effortlessly in the wind currents. There have been sightings as high as four thousand feet, and as much as a thousand miles from land."

"You're kidding," David said.

"The Magnificent has trouble landing on the water. Their feathers and feet are not designed for swimming, so they don't like diving for food."

"Is that why they steal from other birds?" I asked.

"That's their main food supply. And the victims are usually the boobies."

"It's called booby booty," I said. No one noticed.

"The frigates attack the boobies until they disgorge their meals. That's how rough it is up there. And they steal nesting material, the eggs, and even the chicks."

"Those booby eggs are rather large," Heather said. "How do the frigates manage to swallow them?"

"They don't. They puncture the exposed part of the egg with their bills. The hook goes right through the shell."

"I have a neighbor like that," I said.

"What are those red things on their fronts?" Heather asked.

"Gular pouches. During courtship, the males inflate them into taut, red balloons, and then make like bubble dancers."

"That's got to be an exaggeration."

"No, really. The male waits until there's a female overhead. Then he turns his wings skyward, vibrates them, and moves his head from side to side. When she joins him, he dances faster and makes a rattling sound. And he keeps the wing vibrations going all the time. It's quite evocative. It's also out of season. They normally mate in the spring."

"Let's go visit," I said. "I want to be seduced by a frigate."

3. Landing on Tortuga

Peter didn't like the idea. "You'll be interfering."

"With what?" Tui asked. "They won't lay any eggs this time of year."

"What about the schedule?"

Tui ignored him.

Pat jumped out of bed and threw on her clothes. I couldn't rouse Joe. Peter was annoyed.

"What's he going to do, sleep all day? We can't fix breakfast with him in the way."

"So wake him."

Peter didn't reply. He held the dinghy close to the side while we jumped in.

Tui knelt on the bow, rope in hand, camera box slung over her shoulder, directing Hugo to one of the outlying lava rocks. Despite his years of experience, he had trouble getting close enough. Tui's cat-like jump startled me. She made it look simple. I hurried forward and pushed off just as an enormous wave pulled the dinghy back.

"Wait!" she yelled, too late. The water felt colder than I would have expected, and I scraped my knee on the rocks crawling out. Together we pulled the boat back in. I leaned over and grabbed Pat's camera. But the zoom lens she was using made it heavy and awkward, and I almost fell back in.

"Watch what you're doing!" Pat yelled as she crawled up.

"You guys go ahead," Tui said. "I'll wait for the others."

We slogged ashore and regrouped. I was glad Joe had missed the wet landing. It wasn't the kind of scene he enjoyed.

The steep slopes of Tortuga were covered with frigate nests. A few feet above shore line, we were among them. It was a clamorous scene. Males, females, and chicks danced, flapped, squalled, fed, soared, honked, and burbled. The hungry, demanding chicks were the loudest. But it was the males with their remarkable heart-shaped pouches extended who commanded our attention.

Pat crouched behind a bush, camera in hand, looking like a pale but intent frigate. The rest of us followed Tui. The lava rock made it hard going, and my soggy tennis shoes squished at each step.

I was directly behind Tui. "Peter's really upset with Joe, isn't he?"

"He doesn't understand Joe. I'm a little puzzled, myself. Why did he come all this way if he wasn't interested in the Galapagos?"

"Joe's shy. He hasn't traveled a lot. This trip is a big deal. And I think it bothers him that someone else is in charge of his life. At home, he doesn't let that happen."

"I hope they don't come to blows."

"Hey up there, wait a minute!" It was Heather. They had fallen behind. We stood looking at the brilliant colors on the ocean as they labored up.

"Tui, please slow down so we can hear you."

"You mean you missed that?" I said.

"Missed what?" Heather asked.

"Tui was talking about Darwin's work on this island. He lived here for a month, eating frigate bird eggs."

"Actually, we were just rambling on. You didn't miss a thing."

"But did Darwin land here?" Heather insisted.

"Of course not, Heather," David said. "Gwen was being funny."

"What's funny about that?"

I tried to tune them out as I trudged after Tui. We spent about thirty minutes exploring the volcanic slope and disturbing the birds. Tui took three or four pictures, David, about thirty.

When we reached Pat's bush, we found her jubilant. She had waited for the frigates to accept her. Then she could observe them in their natural state.

"You look like a frigate floozy," David said.

"I'm quite taken with one of the males. You guys are so busy racing around, you don't really get acquainted. You're missing all the fun."

4. Tui

Peter set the course for Villamil and told me to get Joe out of bed. I went down to wake him. He wasn't thrilled, but he finally agreed to get up. The sun was hot, but for once we were riding the current rather than bouncing from crest to crest, and Joe wasn't seasick. Tui was steering. I joined her, and we talked casually for a while. Then I said, "I hope you don't think I'm prying, but I wanted to ask about your education. You're so young—"

"I'll turn twenty next week."

"That's what I mean. None of us went off lecturing at nineteen. Where did you go to school?"

"I didn't. My parents taught me. We don't have an extensive library, but they had brought the books they loved most."

"But you're already a published author—"

"You saw my article in OCEANS?"

"Yes. And some of your photographs. How did you learn to take pictures like that?"

"By watching the professional photographers I was guiding. I was sure I could do it. But I needed money to buy a camera. Fortunately, the government had put a bounty on goats."

"Goats?"

"Goats and pigs are a problem. Sailors left them here for food. For the passing ships, it was a God-send. They'd pick up some tortoises for long term storage—"

"That's so cruel!"

"—I know. And they also had fresh milk, and meat from the goats and pigs. But the animals bred like crazy, and soon they were eating up the islands. I'm not overly fond of those animals."

"It's still hard for me to imagine you shooting any animal, let alone a poor little goat."

"You'd kill a chicken, wouldn't you?" I nodded. "Goat's are our chicken. Anyway, I finally earned enough to buy a camera. I was lucky. My pictures were pretty good from the start. It's because I know the animals—how to approach them, what they're going to do."

"That's an amazing story. You could do anything you wanted, couldn't you?"

"We all can."

"Tui, are there any reptiles on Tortuga?" David asked. I left them to it. They deserved their time. Heather had pulled off a fantastic coup. Having Tui for a guide would enhance the trip for all of us. At some point, I'd have to admit that to Heather.

5. Villamil

"This afternoon you'll have a look at Villamil," Peter announced over lunch.

"People live there, right?" I asked.

"True."

"So what's to see?"

"Flamingos in the lagoon, primarily."

That didn't sound too bad. I tried to push aside my bias. Academy Bay was too recent. I didn't want to see more people.

But I did. Ashore, we found ourselves in a typical fishing village. Tui led us to the lagoon which turned out to be a brackish pond inhabited by five flamingos, a duck or two, and a few muddy children from the colony.

"Hey, Gwen, Pat, where are you going?" David called.

"Back to the beach," I replied. "This isn't my idea of excitement."

"So what did you expect?"

"Flamingos," Pat said.

"But they're right here."

"I was expecting Africa. In the Rift Valley, the lakes are covered with thousands of pink birds. When you make a noise, they flap off in pink drifts, floating higher and higher, filling the universe with pink—"

"I hate pink," I commented.

"This isn't Africa," David said.

"You're telling me."

Pat took three or four pictures out of a sense of duty. Back home, we discovered she had captured a beauty neither of us had seen—not only the beauty of the birds, but also the fragile loveliness of the place. It was another example of how tourists push away experience. But this time I was doing it myself. All I could see that day was ugly squalor and a few incongruous, garish birds.

As we headed back to shore, David and Heather continued to cross-examine Tui. "Are the (blank) endemic?" one of them would ask. Tui would give a detailed answer. I enjoyed her responses, but not the questions. Pat, Joe and I walked on ahead.

The beach was flat and white. It seemed to roll slowly under the lapping waves. I took off my shoes and reveled in the feel of the water whooshing in and out. Pat and Joe sat down to rest.

I walked on to a long peninsula of sand that jutted out from the coastline. It was covered with decaying brush and trees, limbs embraced in an elaborate composition. They were long dead, and yet I felt life stir in those used-up pieces of wood. It was Gus' cave all over again, and I was deeply moved.

When I rejoined the group, David was saying, "Pat, what's the reading on your light meter?"

"Where do the gulls nest?" Heather wanted to know.

"I just had the most incredible experience," I said. "Out there on the peninsula— It's life and death all mixed up together, like in Gus' cave—"

"I haven't seen any finches, Tui. Are there none on this island?" Heather went on. "David, get that hawk, see him, on the limb? It's a wonderful shot."

They kept up the chatter, blocking me out, until we were back on board.

6. Fernandina

Peter greeted us with exciting news. "Fernandina is erupting. Tomorrow morning, when we round that point, we'll see her."

"That's incredible," David said.

"I've never been close to an eruption," I said. "Will there be rivers of lava?"

"I want flame," Pat said. "A towering pillar of flame shooting up out of the crater. You do have major eruptions here, I know that. Puenta Espinosa was formed by one."

"What's Puenta Espinosa?" I asked.

"A land formation on Fernandina," Tui said. "It was formed in 1825. We'll be staying there."

"How do we know when it was formed?"

"A ship's captain witnessed it," Pat said. "His description of fire and brimstone is exactly what an eruption should be. It must have been ferocious. It altered the shape of the island."

"So is this a major explosion?" I asked.

"You sound like you want to see. this gorgeous place torn up," Joe said.

"I don't. But if it's going to happen anyway, I don't want to miss it."

Tui was the first to spot Fernandina. "There she is, dead ahead. See those strange cumulus clouds over her?"

Until that moment, we had had a lazy morning. The sea was calm, the sun relaxing. We had been chatting, reading, drinking coffee, dozing. Tui was a marvelous guide, responding to our questions, relating adventures in various parts of the islands, telling us about other tourists she had traveled with.

But news of the eruption had intruded, and our easy relaxed moods were gone. We were filled with anticipation and, at the same time, a little edgy, as if responding to the basic life force of the volcano. It was like being in the presence of an angry god.

I soon became aware that Heather and David were plotting something. They were whispering to one another as they scurried about, digging out maps, questioning Tui. I went looking for Pat.

"What's going on?" I asked.

"They're probably asking questions about the eruption. Why?"

"They're making me nervous."

"Go read a book," she advised.

I found a spot in the shade of the mast, and tried to read. But I couldn't help noticing Heather and David's movements. Eventually they disappeared for a huddle in Peter's quarters.

7. I make a tough decision

They were gone a long time. When they finally emerged, they held a meeting with Peter and Tui in the cockpit. By this time I was really upset. They were replanning the entire trip with the crew before they had even spoken to us about it. It was a replay of the firing incident. I had half a mind to barge into their precious conference, but decided instead to wait them out.

I was fuming when Tui sat down next to me.

"What would you think of adding a small side trip to the schedule?" she asked.

"If Heather and David want a side trip, they can come and talk to me themselves. Why send you?"

"Because they were sure you'd be upset. Now listen a minute. This is a side trip I want very much to make."

"To where?"

"The volcano. I want to climb Fernandina and photograph the crater while it's erupting."

"And this was your idea, right?" I said. "Heather and David had nothing to do with it—"

"Let's keep personalities out of it—"

"You haven't been cooped up with these personalities for the better part of a month—"

"Think of yourself. How many times will you be on hand for an eruption? How often will you be traveling with a guide who can take you there? Don't you want to see it?"

"No, I don't want to see it. These are the same fools who brought us the cockamamie idea of flying down here. We almost killed ourselves once. I made it through that stupidity, and I have no intention of winding up trapped in a lava flow."

"It would be safe. I know a lot about volcanic eruptions—"

"You're out of your mind."

"Possibly. But didn't you tell me a while ago that you admired my ability to deal with the wilderness?"

"I suppose I did."

"Part of dealing with it is not being afraid. And I'm getting the idea you're scared."

"It's not that."

"Then you'll come?"

I stared at the back of Heather's head and thought how good it would feel to wreck her plan. But I couldn't do it. "Yes, all right. I'll go. I just don't like the way they're going about it—"

"Forget them! It was my idea to come talk to you. I want to do this, and we need a majority to overrule Peter. I thought you might listen to me."

"You have my attention."

"We won't have to change the schedule much. We can make it to the crater rim in one day, sleep there, and come back down in the morning."

"And if we're on the rim, we could consider sacrificing Heather and David."

"I hadn't thought of that."

"I'm beginning to like this. Do you really think we can do it?"

"I'm sure of it," Tui replied. "Peter can land us with no trouble at all. There's a wonderful beach area at the end of the channel. We'll have to carry bedrolls and food, but we'll keep it simple."

"But what about Pat? She really can't make that climb."

"Peter will entertain her here."

"Oh, God, she's going to hate this," I groaned.

"Would it help for us to deny our own adventure?"

"No. Not at all. O.K., you win. Sign me on."

Pat was sitting on the bow. I joined her. "We're going to try to climb Fernandina. Tui wants to photograph the crater."

"What a marvelous idea. We'll—" I watched disappointment register on her face. "I can't go, of course. You guys will have a great time."

"I'm sorry. But you'll get some fantastic photos from the boat—"

"Won't that be too thrilling." She turned away. I left her to her thoughts and found David and Heather in the cockpit.

"Will you come?" Heather asked.

"Wouldn't miss it. Thanks for thinking of it."

"It was really Tui's idea."

"I must remember to thank her."

8. An incredible cocktail hour

We stood for a long time, watching the hovering, shifting, undulating cloud over Fernandina.

"Look," Heather gestured toward the volcano, "I think the clouds are getting lighter. We'll be able to see the flames any minute now."

"Sure we will," I said, moving toward Joe who was perched on the cabin roof.

"Heather's right," David said. "The clouds are definitely moving to the left." He handed Heather the binoculars. "The wind must be shifting."

"Let me know when you spot the flames," I shouted back at him. "So, Joe, do you want to climb Fernandina?" I asked.

"Suits me fine. Anything to get off this boat."

"You really hate having someone else in control, don't you?" He laughed. "Right on."

"Hey, Joe, Gwen, come look at this. The clouds are getting thicker," David yelled. "The pressure must be increasing."

I ignored David. "We'll make a sailor out of you yet, Joe."

"Hey, have a look up front," Peter called. "There's a whale trying to lead us to our anchorage."

We gathered on the bow and were awed by the sight before us. The whale was huge. He was moving ahead of the boat, rising and falling above the waves, his enormous bulk invisible most of the time. But when he surfaced or dove, the enormity of the creature made me feel insignificant. We followed him in lazy circles for a long time, watching his every move.

Eventually he tired of the game and dove out of sight.

9. Elizabeth Bay

And then we were surrounded by the magic of Elizabeth Bay. The enormous cactus and rock garden is out of scale: the rocks are the size of small islands, the cactus, tree size. Peter parked in a miniature cove near a small rock pile topped with a tasteful fringe of cactus.

Hugo drove right onto the sandy beach, and we went exploring. Tui and I set a faster pace than the others and soon were alone. She was collecting snails for a scientist friend, and I attempted to help her. We weren't successful, but had a delightful scramble among the rocks and observed an early phase of the sunset from the cliff.

Hugo arrived to pick us up and soon we were comfortably established in the cockpit for cocktail hour. We were all startled by a braying sound close by.

"What the hell is that?" Joe asked.

"Penguins."

"Penguins? Here?"

"Yes. We have a subspecies. They look like miniatures. You'll see some tomorrow. They stand about a half a meter high."

"Look how blue the water is," I said.

"The ocean is generally blue, Gwen," Joe said.

"But it's different in the Galapagos. The blue is more intense. And the water here in Elizabeth Bay is the deepest blue I've ever seen."

I watched the water, then looked up at the sky. I was impatient for the darkness that would highlight the eruption.

But there was nothing, not even a faint tinge of red. Nothing but a soft velvet veil encompassing the boat, the sea, the hanging cactus gardens, and that mysterious pillar of cloud. The stars were dimmed by the nearness of the cloud, but it had no light of its own to outshine them.

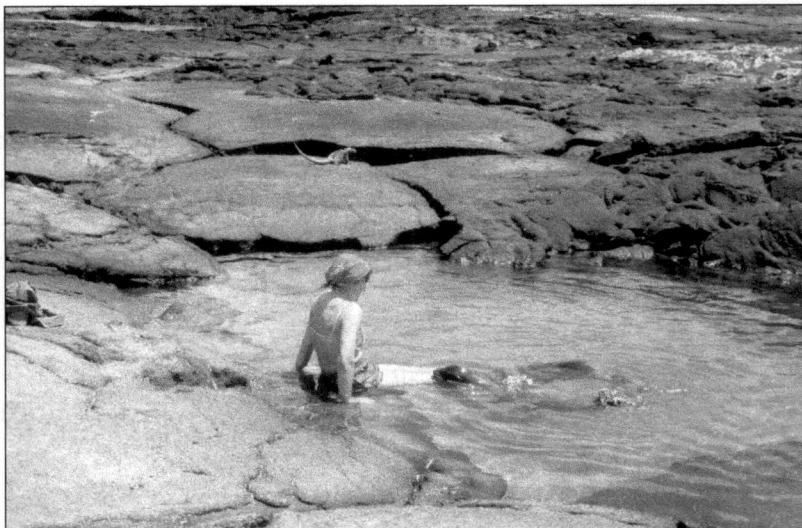

Pat inviting a young fur seal into her lap in a lava pool at Puenta Espinoza.

CHAPTER FIFTEEN
Elizabeth Bay to Puenta Espinosa and beyond

1. A false alarm

I awoke to Peter's shouting: "You should be up and dressed. We have to leave here in five minutes."

"Why?"

He didn't respond. I had no idea where we were going. I draped a sheet around me and slid my feet onto the side of Joe's bunk. He opened his eyes.

"What the hell— You want me to get up?"

"What makes you think that?" I asked.

"Why else would you be standing on my chest?"

I looked down at my feet. "Sorry. Getting in and out of that bunk isn't getting any easier."

"Your aim is terrible."

"You're so smart, you try it." I hopped down. "Peter's upset. Do you know where we're going?"

"No. I slept through his briefing last night."

"You don't suppose this is the day we hike up the volcano—" I put my stuff bag on the stairs and started searching for a sweatshirt.

"No," Joe replied. "We're a long way from Fernandina."

"But what else could it be? You'd better get up if you want to go with us."

When I turned around, Joe was on his feet and fumbling through his duffel bag. "So that's what it takes to get you out of bed."

"I don't want to be left alone on this boat with Peter."

"Here's your jacket. We'll need zinc oxide, Kleenex—"

"Are you people coming or not?" Peter shouted from the deck.

"Aren't you going to wake her?" Joe pointed at Pat.

"She's not coming, remember? You'd better make your bed, Joe. Peter will be furious if you don't."

"Who says I'm not coming?" Pat sat up and rubbed her eyes. "Why didn't someone wake me?"

"But Pat, you can't. You'll get too tired—"

"Nonsense. There are some things that are worth getting tired over, and this is one of them." She disappeared into the head.

We had almost finished packing when Peter yelled, "Hurry it up!"

"What else do I need? Joe, help me."

"Ice skates?"

"Damn it, be serious."

"I wonder if it will be light enough for pictures?" Pat asked.

"You surely aren't going without your camera?"

"You have thirty seconds." Peter sounded angry.

"But we aren't ready."

"—Twenty-nine, twenty-eight—"

"I give up. Let's go."

"But I haven't made my bed—"

We squashed ourselves into the dinghy. "Could someone move their foot off of mine?" Pat asked.

"Sorry." David's shoe scrapped along the bottom of the boat.

"Wait, Peter," I said. "Tui's not here."

"She's sleeping. Like I told you last night, there isn't room for her."

I felt silly. Tui must be coming later, with the bedrolls and food. But that meant we would be landing in the dark without the benefit of her experience. That seemed a bad way to start the climb up Fernandina.

"Tui should be with us," I said.

"I'm sorry to disappoint you, but you'll have to make do with me," Peter replied.

"I didn't mean—" The engine drowned me out. I decided to let it go. Peter had a short fuse these days. On the other hand, he hadn't had more than three hours sleep a night since he picked us up. He had to be exhausted.

The outboard made a terrible racket. I hadn't had my coffee, and I was a little frightened. We weren't properly prepared.

"Look." Pat pointed to the right. In the silver morning light, I thought I saw the outlines of a swamp.

"Peter, is that a swamp over there?" I yelled.

"Of course it's a swamp. Where the bloody hell do you think we're going?"

"I thought—" I paused. "You don't want to know."

"She thought we were going up the volcano this morning," Joe said, then laughed along with the others.

"I told you last night—" Peter ranted. The roar of the outboard made it easy to ignore him.

2. *The mangrove swamp*

Peter turned off the motor and we were in another world. The huge water-bound mangroves were clear in the early light, drooping into the water, stretching their roots forward to conquer new domains. Behind the smaller forward line, they rose to envelop the main channel in an arch of lacy green. We floated into a vaulted passage enclosed by the trees entangled high above us. The dense network of branches hid the rising sun, but light was visible through the leaves.

"Where's the camera, David?" Heather asked.

"I didn't bring it."

"Why not?"

"Because it was dark."

"If you guys don't shut up—" Peter growled.

The water was deep green, glowing, highly reflective. For a long moment, we were motionless as we listened to the intense silence of the swamp. Nothing stirred, not even an insect chirruped. Then, as the sound of our motor drifted out of consciousness, with a single voice, the swamp came alive.

Peter sculled the boat into the channel where we met our first turtle. We spotted his outline below the surface, then a blunt head poked through the water, creating a spreading series of sparkling ripples. When he saw us, he glided off with a superb grace of motion unexpected in such an ungainly form.

I was enchanted. I also noticed that I smelled. I announced this to my friends.

"I could have told you that," Joe laughed.

"It's the heat," Peter said. "Clothes age fast in equatorial climates. There's something about the residual salt water and the humidity that causes material to disappear."

"But what causes the smell?" I asked.

"The mold. It's the stench of decay."

"Good God. I hope it's just the clothes."

"We'll let you know," Peter replied.

Suddenly we came upon a net suspended in the water across the channel. It was attached to trees on either side. A single turtle had wound his flippers through it and was struggling valiantly to escape.

"He's all right," Peter said. "A scientist at the Darwin Station is doing a study. He'll be along in a while. He wants to examine the turtles."

"What a nice guy," I said. "Has he ever spent the night floundering in a net?"

"Oh come on, Gwen. That turtle doesn't know the difference," David said.

"May you be reincarnated as a butterfly."

"Keep up the chatter if you want to scare off every animal in the swamp," Peter said.

We had reached a dead end. Peter turned the boat, surprising a large turtle who had been following us at a safe distance. He disappeared under water.

We soon found a second side passage, this one somewhat less densely overgrown. Here, the sunlight penetrated. The leaves of the mangroves were outlined in glowing fire, creating a green world. The emerald water turned to jewels where it was struck by sunlight.

"We should have brought the camera," Heather said.

"Well, we didn't. Next time we'll—"

"There won't be a next time if I have anything to do with it," Peter said.

A group of sea lions swam out from a side channel to cavort around the boat. They somersaulted and chased their tails. We were one of the more entertaining events of the day. They seemed more leisurely and playful, less competitive, than their colleagues on the beaches. A small group formed an escort, following us at a short distance, occasionally putting on a burst of speed, darting around the boat, diving forward and surfacing to laugh at us. A pair of penguins, more cautious and sober, swam out to check on us. Others watched from shore. And the trees, the water, the sky were alive with birds of all kinds, adding their song to the invisible chorus of the swamp.

Finally, when we had explored every corridor, we turned back toward the Bronzewing. I hadn't realized the importance of the reef in protecting the intimate atmosphere of the swamp. But now, looking beyond it to the open sea, the free, multicolored external world was in sharp contrast.

At the entrance, we spotted a great blue heron, nesting in a small tangle of mangroves. The regal bird seemed to float on the top of branches too frail to support her weight. Staring disdainfully at us from her tree top that rose a few feet out of the water, she was symbolic of the islands: stunning, lonely, and unlikely.

As we neared the boat, I looked back across the reef and into the channel. It was guarded on each side by sculpted rocks.

"It's the entrance to paradise," I said to Pat.

"No. It's the gates of dawn."

3. Puenta Espinosa

For the next two days, we continued on course, making our way between Fernandina and Isabella. We parked in beautiful, serene bays, but none of us enjoyed it the way we would have a few days earlier. Our thoughts were on the climb, and our eyes were drawn to the large cloud bank hovering over the volcano.

Finally we crossed to Fernandina and went ashore at Puenta Espinosa. Almost all of the Galapagos creatures live here—sea lions, pelicans, hawks, doves, oyster catchers, herons, flightless cormorants, penguins, boobies, and thousands of marine iguanas.

It is the iguanas and cormorants who greet you. They are an integral part of the vast expanse of barren lava. The black rock has been broken into an intricate network of reefs by the constant battering of verdant sea water.

A dense grove of mangroves rises like a backdrop to one side. Tui led us there first, to explore the shadowy nooks. And then we walked along the scattered coral beaches. There were sea lions everywhere.

"Go on into the water," Tui said. "It's perfectly safe to swim with them."

Indeed, they were charming companions, diving around us as if inviting us to play, watching us closely, laughing at our awkwardness. They were curious about us, but totally unafraid.

Pat was sitting at the edge of a tide pool, taking pictures of a mother with young, when one of the babies scrambled into her lap.

Then we walked slowly along the vast lava flow. This place seemed at once new and old. I felt as if I'd come home. All of the Galapagos, but especially Puenta Espinosa, triggered a memory forgotten. It was familiar, the pungent, sweet smell of the swamp, the curious acceptance of other creatures— It was known. We had lost it somewhere.

"Tui," Heather said, "Is it true those cormorants can't fly?"

"Yes. Their wings have evolved into small stumps. There are still a few feathers. The breastbones don't have keels. Most people think they evolved this way because there's so much food available, they have no need to fly. And of course there are no predators."

"I can't believe how awkward they are," Pat said.

"On land, yes. But they're graceful when they swim."

"Until they dive," Joe said. "Look— Bottoms up!"

"What's he doing?" David pointed at a cormorant parent who was standing in the sun, his small wing-stumps extended.

"Most birds spread their wings like that in the sun—it dries the feathers and also provides air conditioning on a hot day."

"Someone should tell them those fuzzy stumps aren't wings."

"What's that chick doing?" David pointed at an enormous young bird who was shrieking forlornly. One of the adults approached and the chick plunged it's head deep into the parent's throat.

"Don't tell me he's eating."

"That's about it."

All of us sat there for a long time. I was touched by the caring behavior of the cormorant family, warmed by the sun reflected from the lava formations, thrilled by the magic of the place. But as Hugo rowed us back to the Bronzewing, my thoughts returned to the volcano. We sat in the cockpit with our drinks and watched a dazzling sunset. The inferno over Fernandina was changing, and we talked in hushed voices of getting closer to it.

4. The crunch

We set out early toward the volcanic clouds. The billowy masses were moving rapidly, and we tracked every change. Meanwhile, preparations for the climb were underway. Tui was making sandwiches and filling water bottles.

"You'd better get your backpacks ready." She handed me a water bottle. "It won't be long now."

I had filled my backpack and was tying my sleeping bag in place when David came below.

"We're almost to the open sea, and its rough out there. Bring your stuff on deck. When we're ready to land, we'll have to move fast."

"What are you going to do about your blisters?"

"Walk on them," David replied.

"That sounds dangerous."

"I will not let a little sunburn keep me from getting to the top of that volcano."

"David, are you coming?"

"We're on our way."

I had only been below for a few minutes, so I was astonished at the change in the sea. We had left the sheltered channel between Isabella and Fernandina, and were now in a rolling ocean with whitecaps whipped by the wind. We had driven right into the clouds that encircled the volcano and could feel their dampness on our cheeks.

Peter turned the Bronzewing. "The landing beach is that-a-way. We should be able to lower the dinghy in five minutes."

I studied the shoreline. One rock formation stood out like a lighthouse. Its rocks seemed to have been fitted together by a giant and left as a reminder of his presence. I wondered what it would look like from the other side. But then I noticed that we weren't getting any closer.

"Peter, what's going on?" I asked. "We don't seem to be moving."

"We aren't. We have the wind and the tide against us. This engine wasn't meant to go upstream."

"Peter," Tui said, "Maybe we should follow the coast for a bit and then turn back this way. That would put the wind behind us—"

"Right. We'll give it a try."

Joe emerged from the cabin. "How are you feeling?" I asked.

"Fine. No sign of seasickness this time. I guess I finally passed the test."

"The test comes when it's time to land," Peter said grimly.

"But Tui said landing would be easy."

"Not in these seas, it won't. And Joe here hasn't bothered to practice."

"Come on, Peter," Joe said. "What do I need to practice?"

"You'll have to tell me after you've landed with wet gear— Oh God, look at the size of that baby—"

An enormous wave rose before us and crashed on the bow. Pat stood up shakily and started down the steps. "Your camera—"

"Wet again. I can't even take pictures—" She disappeared.

"I'll have to try another approach," Peter shouted.

"Is that the only place we can land?" Heather asked Tui.

"Just about. Normally we have no trouble getting in there. I don't know why we're being so unlucky today."

Peter tried several different angles, but each time had to turn back when the surf started heaving us about.

"Let's take the dinghy in from here," Heather suggested.

"It's much too rough for that," Peter replied. "Heavy seas like this would swamp you in no time."

"But the dinghy's more maneuverable—"

"No way! Forget it!"

"Listen, Peter," David said, "If you're worried about Heather's not being able to swim, I can take care of her."

"Heather can't swim?" Peter shouted.

"It's not a problem." Heather wet her lips. "But I'm thinking of taking it up when I get back home."

"Not a problem?" Peter's face was red. "God damn it all to hell, would you really let someone who can't swim get into a dinghy on this open sea?"

"I told you," David said. "I can take care of her. She's my responsibility."

"No, she is not. The whole damn lot of you is my responsibility, and mine alone. I'm supposed to be smart enough to avoid messes like this."

"Let's not overreact," Heather said. "If we wait an hour or so, we'll be able to get in close."

"Fine. So we get you landed. And then tomorrow we can't get you off the damned island. How's that for a scenario?"

Peter positioned the tiller for a long sweeping turn. "Tui, did you know this? Did you know Heather can't swim?"

"No. But I still think we'd be all right in a calm ocean."

"And what would you do about getting back to the boat?"

"You worry too much, Peter."

"Where are you going?" David asked.

"To Puenta Albamarle and on to James. This little adventure is over."

"We made it from Guayaquil in a single engine plane," David protested.

"I don't know how I forgot that, but thanks for reminding me. I know better than to take advice from idiots."

"It's my risk, not yours," Heather said.

"Let it go, Heather," David said. "Peter's in charge of the boat."

I took my backpack below and found Pat sitting on her bunk.

"I'm sorry," she said. "I hated being left behind, but I'm sorry you guys aren't going."

"That's called mixed feelings. I'm pretty disappointed, but it would have been terrifying to see Heather go overboard. I suspect Peter's right."

"Undoubtedly," she agreed.

5. I dream of canaries

David's reminder about the plane registered in my unconscious, and that night I dreamed we were back in Guayaquil having engine problems. We were flying a plane with two engines that were powered, not by gas, but by canaries. The problem was that they had to fly counter-clockwise. We needed some new birds and the only ones available were clockwise. I was, naturally, distraught.

I related the dream over breakfast and put it out of my mind. The next day Peter announced that he, too, had dreamed about the plane. Pat had been acting as pilot, and he was the terrified passenger. They had flown into Quito. It was night when they arrived and, fascinated by the neons on the main street, she had flown the plane down the steep hill, under the lights.

The following night, Pat dreamed that we were back in Los Angeles, but that we had to return to the Galapagos via commercial jet because we'd forgotten to bring the plane home.

Whether we were talking in our sleep or not, there was something contagious about the flight dreams, and each morning a different member of the group related one. It pleased me enormously to learn that Hugo had entered into the group activity. According to Peter's edited translation, Hugo had taken the plane so that he could visit his lady friends on the mainland. He had managed the flight well enough, but the landing in Guayaquil had given him problems. The rest of his adventures were apparently satisfactory, if his giggles when questioned, were any indication.

CHAPTER SIXTEEN
James Bay to Baltra

1. A rough ride

I was on my way below when Peter yelled, "We're skipping the lunch stop. There's more rough weather ahead."

"I don't think the others will be eating," I replied. "Not in this surf. And we still have Tui's sandwiches."

"Hugo made ceviche," Pat added.

We had to hang onto our plates and cups, but Tui, Pat, Hugo and I enjoyed our meal.

Back on deck, the movement of the boat made it hard to read, but it was fun being in the sun, feeling the wind on our faces, and the excitement of plowing through those gigantic waves. It wasn't until eight o'clock, when we were cold and damp, that I became bored with the whole thing. I went below and found a sweatshirt, then sat down in the cockpit with Peter.

"Does it always take this long to get to James?"

"No way," Peter said. "Everything's going against us tonight—the current, the wind— Look how the ocean's churning out there—"

"It's tossing us around like a rubber duck."

"We need the sail. Tui, take the tiller," Peter ordered. "Hugo—" The two of them hurried to raise the enormous white sail. It was a struggle with the boat bouncing around crazily. We were in the way.

"I thought I told you guys to go below."

"O.K., if you insist." Joe stood up just as the boom slammed to the opposite side. The heavy beam glanced off the side of his head. He sat down with a thud.

"That's why I don't want you here." Peter rushed back to the cockpit to examine Joe. "Doesn't seem to have broken the skin. Are you O.K.?"

"Why wouldn't I be? Nothing like a blow to the head to make you feel great."

"I'll fix coffee." I stumbled down the steps, happy for an excuse to get out of there. David and Joe joined me. "The bunks on the downside are sleepable," David said, "And I'm claiming one of them."

"Peter says I can use his bunk." Heather was behind me in the cabin.

"Joe's already in bed. So the three downhill bunks are taken. Pat, what are you doing?"

"Getting into bed," she said.

"But your bunk is on the upside. You'll fall out."

"I'll put my hand against the table."

"You're going to hold yourself in bed while sleeping?"

"There's nothing to it," she snapped.

I poured two cups of instant coffee and carried them slowly toward the steps. Hugo was in his bunk, apparently defying the laws of gravity as he slept.

"Thanks," Peter said. "I needed something about now."

"It looks calmer."

"It is. The wind in the sail has a stabilizing effect."

"I see," I said. "So we're holding steady at a forty degree list."

"Make that twenty, but yes."

Tui carried her bedroll down the steps and spread it out on the cabin floor.

I looked across the cockpit at Peter. "Would you mind if I sat here a while? I don't want to be in the way."

"You're not. It's when the whole lot of you starts jumping around the cockpit that I can't take it. Not when the weather's this tricky."

"We're a bit much any time."

He laughed. "Sorry I've been in such a bad mood."

"You're tired."

"It's not that. I was bloody well scared out of my mind when I realized you idiots were planning to take a woman who can't swim out on that ocean."

"We seem to have lost touch with reality somewhere over Panama."

"That's what gets me about this job. If you let your attention stray for one moment, the worst happens."

"So why do you keep doing it?"

He stared at the ocean for a long time. "I suppose it's because, deep down, I love it. How else would I get to see this place? And there are times when it's peaceful—like it will be when Tui takes those two up Alceda."

"You'd have even more peace if we all got out of your way."

"Don't apologize. I'd do the same thing in your place."

We fell silent as the boat heeled into the water. The sky was dark with clouds and mist, the ocean visible only in ringlets of spray. I stayed there a long time, tasting the wind, the cold, the night. I felt free, as if my life had moved off hold.

2. James

Peter parked in a protected bay on James Island, and we had a delightfully quiet evening. In the morning we made an easy dry landing and followed Tui across an extensive, rough lava flow. The lava was scarified with fissures that filled up as the surf came in only to be emptied immediately. The heavy sound of water falling on rock echoed over the usual pounding of the waves.

"Can we stop here, Tui?" Heather asked. "This is a beautiful place for pictures."

"Let's go on a little farther. You'll love the fur seal grotto. When it's calm, I go swimming with them."

We were delighted to find not one grotto, but a huge complex of them. We stumbled around on the interconnecting lava, almost tripping over fur seals who watched us with large, dark eyes.

Their plush coats were roughed up where they had been scratched with a back flipper. They were curious about us and, if we stayed still, came close for a better look. After the enormous sea lions, the fur seals seemed petite.

"Over here," Pat called. "I found the central grotto."

I climbed down to the spot and stood admiring the two rock arches below. The heavy surf was causing water to whoosh under the arches and into the rear of one of the grottos where it hit the back wall and rose in an enormous spume. A few feet farther back, a blow hole caught the final energy and sent an even higher spume into the air.

"Look," David said. "That fur seal's going down."

We watched in amazement as the little creature disappeared head first into the blow hole.

"You said you'd been swimming here, didn't you, Tui?" Pat asked.

"Yes, but not in weather like this."

"I'd like to go in," Pat said.

Tui stared at her.

"I know what you're thinking," Pat said. "But I'm a good swimmer. I trained for the Olympics when I was a kid. Besides, the ocean's pretty calm today."

"You're out of your mind—" Tui protested.

"On the contrary," she replied. "I'm trying to cope. I can't go up Alceda with you tomorrow. I can't go on the hikes. But I can swim better than any of you. I need my adventure. Don't deny me this."

Tui nodded. "I hear you." She paused. "I suppose it's O.K.. Be careful."

"Joe, do you believe this?" I asked. He shrugged and laughed.

Pat dove into the turbulent waters and disappeared.

"Where'd she go?" Joe asked.

"She's up there," David pointed to a wall of lava.

"She's been swept under the arch." Heather was standing on the far edge of the grotto, pointing down. "Now she's coming into the upper pool. She's being tossed around like a leaf—"

We ran around the lava overhang to Heather's side and stared down into a cylindrical hole. One moment it filled with surging water, the next, almost emptied as the current pulled back.

"Is there a way out of this grotto?" I asked.

"No," Tui replied. "Unfortunately, she's going to have to get back under the arch."

"No way," I said.

"She doesn't have a choice," Tui replied. "Pat," she yelled, "Watch that rock behind you—"

"Tui, how can she possibly get back?" David asked.

"By swimming hard. She'll make it."

"She could be killed," David pointed out. "Look how that swell is tossing her back onto the rock—"

"It's a question of timing. She's got to catch the water as it goes down. I think, yes— This time she can do it. "Get ready, Pat. Take a big breath." She paused for a beat. "NOW!" Tui screamed. "GO NOW!"

For a moment, we thought Pat had made it through the arch. But another powerful swell came in, and as it receded, it threw her back against the wall. The water drained out, and Pat was left treading water by the wall of lava.

"Are you O.K.?" Tui called.

"Just out of breath," Pat managed to reply.

"O.K.," Tui coached, "that was close. Now get ready, and when I tell you, go for it." Tui stood on the edge, watching the rise and fall of the surf. Suddenly her body tensed. "Take a breath, Pat, and GO!"

Pat disappeared as the water drained under the arch, and for a moment we couldn't see her at all.

"She's here," Joe shouted. "She made it through."

"Thank God!" Tui said as we all hurried back to help David pull Pat out of the water.

"Pat, are you all right?"

"I'm great," she said between gasps for air. "It was fantastic. As soon as I get my breath, I'm going back in."

"Wait until the heavier swells have passed," Tui said.

"How much of an adventure do you need?" Heather asked.

"I guess you're right." Pat sat down on the side of the pool to wait, and we moved away to watch the fur seals. We heard her cry out when a large wave came crashing in. It caught her, knocked her onto her back and dragged her along the sharp lava, leaving her there in a heap.

We rushed to help.

"Stay away from those waves," I cautioned.

"I'm O.K.," she replied, embarrassed. "Really."

"You're sure?" Tui asked. "You're kind of bloody."

"I'm fine."

"But you can't go back in," Heather said. "It's much too rough."

"No, I suppose not. But God, it was great!"

3. Freedom

We dropped the climbers on the shore of Isabella at ten the next morning, and had two glorious, serene days to explore James. We moved in slow motion, watching flamingos in the lagoon, examining the red and grey rock formations in Buccaneer Cove, talking to Peter.

And we sailed. The Bronzewing reacted like a freed colt. We slipped silently through the water, listening to the wind and the birds, watching the dolphins who were riding our wake, luxuriating in our freedom. There were only four of us to compete for the head and room at the table, let alone the limelight, and Hugo didn't speak English.

On the second evening, Peter invited me to go fishing with him. I was delighted. A school of bonito were swirling around the boat, and I was sure we'd catch several. But Hugo didn't want me to go. He told Peter, in Spanish, that women scare fish away.

Peter translated for me, then said, "Nonsense, Hugo. Come on, Gwen."

We started out in the dinghy, ignoring Hugo's taunts, and soon were moving right over the amazing mass of bonita. Peter gave me the line and we started trolling. I was unhappy with my first catch—a poisonous spiny grouper that Peter threw back. But I figured everyone was entitled to one mistake. Then he started yelling at me and I couldn't figure out why. When I didn't react, he reached the length of the dinghy, grabbed the line, and jerked it frantically just as a blue-footed booby hit the bait.

"Ohmigod," I exclaimed, "I didn't see him coming."

"That was obvious," he grumbled as he hauled the line in. "I think I got it in time." The squawking bird fought him, but soon Peter had the boobie in hand. We were relieved to find that the hook had lodged in the bird's webbed foot, not the body. I held the boobie while Peter removed the hook. The blue feet were magical—warm to the touch and much too big to be believed. No wonder they are used for incubating eggs.

Finally, we let the bird go. He flapped off happily, squawking loudly as he told his friends about his mistreatment.

Peter and I continued trolling for almost an hour, but never caught a single fish despite the incredible mass of them all around us.

Disappointed, we returned to the Bronzewing. I was concerned that we wouldn't have anything to eat for dinner, but I shouldn't have worried. Hugo had already started cooking spaghetti.

4. The hikers return

The next morning we picked up Tui, Joe, Heather and David. They were high from their experience. On the floor of the crater, they had witnessed giant tortoises mating, seen many hatchlings, and watched the adults sunning themselves. David had suffered with his sunburned feet, but he insisted it had been worth it.

I had thought the separation would ease the tensions in the group, but if anything, they were worse. We'd all enjoyed our brief taste of freedom. The next two days were to be an odd mixture of quick stops at entrancing places and short caustic exchanges.

It was almost dusk when we pulled into the Bartholome Islets. Arrow Rock, the majestic obelisk that guards the Islets, already had the glow of dusk around it. Peter had told us about the National Park rules: all tourists must be on board their vessels by dusk. We knew when we pulled in that there really wasn't time for the climb. But we were eager to see the view from the top.

"We're late," Peter yelled. "If you want to go, move fast. Now."

Hugo pulled the dinghy around and tried to help us in. Not wanting to miss this great opportunity, I swung my leg over the side too fast. A swell caused the dinghy to swerve, and I fell, landing on top of Hugo.

He laughed so hard I wondered if he had set me up, but it didn't matter. I was in a great mood as we set off.

It was an easy dry landing, and we were ready to go.

"If you want to do this, we'll have to move fast," Tui said.

"We aren't about to miss it," David said.

"What about you, Pat?"

"I'll just take my time. You go on ahead."

Tui and I raced up the trail with David, Heather and Joe close behind. And then we were on top of the Arrow, looking back toward the island. Sunset had devoured the daylight colors. The island had become a dark mass in the dusky violet water. It was a study in blue and black shapes. I sat down on a rock and wrapped my arms around my knees. I wanted to stay there for the night.

"What the hell setting will we use?" David shouted behind me.

I was annoyed, but decided to ignore him.

"Where's Pat? She's the only one who understands these things." He stepped in front of me and began to adjust his lens.

"I'm sitting here, you oaf," I said.

"This is the best place for the shot I want. Won't be a minute."

"Get out of my view," I shouted. He didn't budge. The temptation of his legs planted firmly in front of me was too much. I grabbed an ankle and shook hard.

For a moment he was off balance. His arms flailed as he fought for control. And then he scrambled back to the path where he stood shaking his fist at me. "You Goddamned idiot! I almost fell down the side of the cliff."

"What a shame. I should have pushed."

"If you two are finished," Tui snapped, "We'd better get back. It's almost dark." Not waiting for a reply, she set off down the trail at a rapid pace.

5. A celebratory dinner

We drove back in silence, but everyone cheered up when we realized that Hugo had made our favorite ceviche for dinner. We had our customary warm rum drinks and peanuts in the cockpit, then went below to eat.

The ceviche was, as always, magnifico!, and Hugo had baked a cake. To celebrate Christmas Eve, Peter opened a bottle of local orange wine. It had a strange metallic taste, but it came with a remarkable story. The wine had been made by Mrs. Whitmore, the woman on San Cristobal whose dentist husband had died mysteriously years before. Peter regaled us all evening with tales of Dr. Whitmore's disappearance and other strange happenings in the Galapagos colony. Thanks to Peter, we forgot our differences and managed to have a pleasant evening.

It was a beautiful, clear night and not too cool. Pat and I decided to join Tui sleeping on deck. She had told us we were really missing it, not sleeping under the stars, and this quiet protected spot seemed a perfect place to try it.

I didn't have much time to enjoy the star show. Relaxed by the rocking boat and the celebratory dinner, I dozed off almost immediately. Sleeping in the open air, out of snore range, was a treat. But we gave up around four. Raindrops were one thing, waves over the bow, quite another.

6. Daphne

We were driving along, having a relaxed morning, when Peter shut down the motor in front of a rather small rock in the middle of the ocean. "This is Daphne," he said. "It's a tiny volcanic structure, one of the smallest of the Galapagos Islands, but well worth seeing."

"How on earth are we going to do that?" I asked. "We couldn't possibly land there. We'll just roll right back into the water."

"Just be careful. It'll be a wet landing, but there are good footholds on the rock. And you only have to climb up about ten feet."

"I think I'll take the morning off," Joe said.

"What's the matter with you?" Peter sounded angry. "Are you afraid of getting wet?"

"No. It just looks pretty slippery on that rock, and I don't feel like risking it."

"For God's sake, Joe," Peter chided. "I've landed an eighty-year-old grandmother here."

Peter had no impact on Joe, but he did get to Pat. She was determined to prove she could deal with the landing as well as an eighty-year-old.

Hugo loaded us into the dinghy and pulled up to the side of the cliff. The ocean was rough, and the movement of the tiny boat didn't help. We were, after all, landing on a small, volcanic uprising in the middle of the ocean.

Still, I was surprised how hard it was to get from the boat to the rock. Only Hugo's hand on my arm kept me from falling in. I ran my hand over the rough surface of the rock and finally located the hollowed-out handholds. The footholds were right below. Once I had pulled myself up onto the cliff, the climb to the first rest spot wasn't bad.

But Pat found it tough. "You go on," she panted. "I'll wait here."

We started to climb and immediately came upon masked boobies. With their love of cliffs, they had found the outer shell of the volcano an ideal nesting spot. We passed many nests, a few with unhatched eggs, some with fluffy young birds peeping out from under sleek adults, more with large gawky chicks nervously awaiting food.

The rim was unbearably hot and barren, and I was relieved when we started down into the crater. The flat floor of the crater was covered with blue-foots. There were thousands of them. They squawked, flapped, landed, dove, and fought, carrying out their own complete social life in that desolate environment.

We didn't stay long. The heat and smell were hard to take, and we hurried back to the rim. On the way back down, Tui and I stopped several times to wait for Heather and David.

"What will you do for adventure, now that you know the islands so well?" I asked.

"I love it here. Every time out is an adventure."

"I mean a real adventure. Like the time you were lost on Isabella. That couldn't happen to you now. You know too much."

"You can't know too much. But I have a theory about adventure. If you're lucky, like I was, they happen to you while you're young. Once you have the taste for them, you learn to make them happen."

"How so?"

"Well, in my case, I'm planning to take my rowboat to Barrington," she replied.

"You want to row there from Academy Bay?"

"Yes. Don't you think that would be adventure?"

"I'm sorry I asked."

"Listen. We can hear Joe and Peter."

"You're right." I looked below. Peter was driving the Bronze-wing back and forth offshore, talking to Joe who had stretched out on the roof of the cabin. We could hear their conversation as if they were standing next to us. Fortunately, they were discussing nothing more personal than the overflight of Fernandina we would attempt that afternoon.

I told Tui I was dreading the flight back home. "I wish I could simply BE there. There's been enough closeness with these people. I want to be back among my own surroundings."

"Can't you simply go there in your head? That's what I do in situations like that."

"Sometimes, yes. But a week is a long time to run off that way."

"You ought to be able to handle it," she said.

I found it frustrating that, at half my age, Tui seemed in so many ways much wiser than I.

7. Lunch

During our lunch stop, I decided to wash my hair. We'd been cleaning up by swimming with our clothes on and then doing a drip dry. It worked well except for hair. I couldn't get a comb through it. I didn't want to return to civilization wearing a mat, so I decided to rub some shampoo into it before diving in.

The water felt wonderful. I swam around and around the boat, luxuriating in the sweetness of the warm Galapagos current. Then I toweled my hair dry and tried to comb it. I was mortified to discover I had produced steel wool. The comb wouldn't even go through the ends. Pat tried to help, then Joe.

"Ouch! That hurts!"

"I give up," he said. "You'd better shave it off."

"Here, let me," David said. To my surprise, his hands were gentle. He spent a long time untangling the worst of the mess.

Heather came up from below and stood watching, her hands on her hips. "Well, I see you have a new skill."

"He's marvelous," I said. "I'm really grateful, David."

"I'm sure you are. David, I can't find the last roll of film."

"Go ahead." I stood up. "You're fantastic." I moved forward to give him a hug and he backed away. Heather looked at me triumphantly and led him below.

"Hands off, Gwen, remember?" Joe laughed.

"I just wanted to say thank you."

"Have you ever heard of a handshake?" Pat asked.

8. The overflight

It was mid-afternoon when we climbed aboard the old Baltra wagon and headed for the airfield. Joe was nervous about the plane, but it was right where we'd left it. David and Joe spent a couple of hours transferring fuel from the barrels into a bucket and through a chamois into the wing tanks. Heather and I took turns holding the chamois in place.

"There's still quite a bit of gas in the barrel," Joe said. "We can have a nice long flyover."

"Joe, do you think the clouds will lift?" I asked.

"Not here. But maybe we'll be lucky around Fernandina."

Since we'd had nothing but clouds in that area all week, I wasn't too hopeful.

David removed the gas container and the middle seat so that three of us could cram together on the floor. I volunteered to sit between Tui and Peter. That meant I would have absolutely nothing to hold onto. Heather and Pat were in back, Joe and David up front. We were ready.

Joe's takeoff was smooth. The weather had not improved. Most of the way out, we were over the clouds.

"When are you going down?" I shouted at Joe.

"I think I'll wait until we see a peak. The clouds are pretty low today." He was thrilled to be in control again.

"Does he really know what he's doing?" Peter asked me.

"We found the islands, didn't we? He's a wonderful pilot."

"Then why do I feel sick?"

"Because this is your first flight in a small plane. It's more comfortable if you have a seat."

"I'll remember to ask for one next time."

"Let's see if this plane can still move," Joe said.

"Now wait a minute," I yelled. "We are not strapped in back here—"

But Joe was determined. He didn't exactly do loops, but close enough to it that I was sliding from side to side and forward to back.

"God damn it to hell, what are you doing?" I screamed.

"Going under the clouds," he called back.

"Are we upside down?" Tui asked.

She had been very quiet. When I turned to look at her, I was surprised by her pallor.

"To be honest, I don't know. Joe, where are we? Do you know?"

"We're close to Fernandina," he replied. "Let's go have a look." He put the plane into a steep dive to get below the remaining scattered clouds.

"Look, there's the ocean!" Pat shouted.

"That's not water," David yelled. "That's the inside of Alceda."

As the mist cleared, we could see one wall of the volcano straight ahead. "For God's sake, Joe, get us out of here," David screamed.

Joe pulled back on the stick and the plane responded beautifully. I watched the sides of the volcano as we flew past, aware now that we might have died right there. It was a sobering experience.

Soon we were high above the clouds. We flew in silence. I cast sidelong glances at my companions. They were both miserable. They made it back to Baltra without throwing up, but I don't think it was easy.

9. Last night

Tui's father, Andre, joined us for dinner that night. He had hiked across Santa Cruz and caught a ride to Baltra. He would return to Academy Bay with Peter and Tui. Before dinner, we sat over drinks and talked. A gentle, self-contained man, Andre was unshaven. Even dressed in tired shorts and an old shirt, he had great dignity.

"When did you come to the Galapagos?" David asked.

"Shortly after World War II," he replied. "When it was much more isolated."

"You must hate all these tourists," Pat said.

"It's not only the tourists. Oh, the scientists are wonderful people. I have many friends at the Darwin Station. But they get caught up in their own projects, and that makes them intrusive. I don't mean their impact on the environment. They try to keep that down. I mean on our daily lives. They don't use common sense, and that's a worry to all of us. Just the other day, two of them decided they wanted to photograph Fernandina while it was erupting. So they talked a friend into giving them a ride, and then took off in their dinghy. Well, the damned thing was swamped and they went overboard, backpacks and all."

"Are they O.K.?" David asked.

"Just barely. One guy got right back into the dinghy, but getting the other one out of the water was tough. He had to be resuscitated. He's recovered, but what a terrible chance they took."

"Yes. People do the damndest things," Peter said.

I thought it would be nice to change the subject. "I admire you so much," I said, "Seeking out this wilderness, learning to live with it—"

"It will soon be gone. What we came for—the beauty, the isolation—what we came for is being destroyed. I don't think we will find it anywhere else. You see, by now we require such complete freedom. This place has ruined us. We expect wildness, adventure, quiet. We need it. And that need makes us vulnerable."

We listened in awe as he told of adventures on the island. He is living proof that we become our lifestyles. He had remained aloof from the crutches of Western civilization while keeping abreast of ideas. He had chosen the best, and used it well.

10. Take off

The next morning, we hurried through our preparations and were ready for takeoff at nine-thirty. We stood awkwardly by the plane, no one knowing what to say. Everyone shook hands except me. I still hadn't learned to do that and insisted on hugging everyone in sight. We thanked them for an incredible experience, then climbed aboard.

And then we were on our way home. It seemed so anti-climactic. The motor had started instantly, we had all the gas we needed, and there was no chance at all that we would miss the mainland. The adventure was ending, but what an adventure it had been.

As we soared above the islands, I thought about Andre and Tui, and Gus' cave, and Peter and George, and the fur seals— The people, the environment, the experience of being there had made an indelible impression on each of us. We had changed. Pat's dream had become our reality and we would never be the same again.

EPILOGUE

The adventure ended with our return to Guayaquil. I knew Tui's advice was right, that I should simply go home in my head. But the tensions between us were too great. We all had vested interests in the neurotic tangle we had woven.

We were beset by delays. David heard a rumor that gas was scarce in Panama. We wasted half a day trying to find out more, then decided to go check it out in person. On route, we hit a rock on the Buenaventura runway and damaged the hydraulic system. We limped into Panama International, where David spent the better part of a morning borrowing tools and parts from the major airlines to fix it.

I spent most of the morning plotting how to get home via commercial flight. But in the end, I didn't have the heart to desert the others. We talked management out of enough gas to reach northern Panama, and we flew on to the city of David.

I cheered up a little when we had our first warm showers in a month. We had a good dinner and, the next morning, filled up the tanks and our plastic friend just in case we ended up back in Nicaragua.

I thought our problems were over, but we reached our nadir in Acapulco. It was New Year's Eve and no accommodations were available. We asked permission to sleep in the airport lounge, then packed our valuables in the plane. David and Heather picked a lock and sneaked onto the roof to sleep. I disapproved, and told them so. They thought I was being silly. We waited for the poker game in the lounge to break up. When it didn't, Pat and I found couches in the corner and went to sleep with Joe on the floor between us.

As I dozed off, I thought about how righteous I would feel when Heather and David were arrested. They were taking such a ridiculous chance.

But I changed my mind when I awoke to find someone lifting the cushion under my head and feeling around for a wallet. I pretended to be asleep and waited until the robber had left the area. The poker game was still going on. When I was sure the man was gone, I woke Joe and Pat.

"So big deal," Pat said. "Our stuff's in the plane."

I poked Joe in the ribs.

"What the hell—"

"Joe, someone tried to rob me. Just now."

Joe got half up off the floor and felt in his pocket. The plane keys were there. "Not to worry," he said, and fell back to sleep. I spent the rest of the night stewing and wishing, not for the first time, that I'd taken Heather's advice.

The fact that she had been right again didn't make it any easier for me to deal with her. She and David wanted to take extra time on the return trip. They were interested in everything. Joe, Pat and I were eager to get on with our lives. We had settled into a dissonance that lasted far beyond the trip.

But we did, in fact, make it back to the Santa Monica airport on schedule. We called Alan, and he arrived at the airport with the dogs.

"Alan, we're home!" I said, hugging him fiercely.

"Yes, I see that."

"Well, aren't your surprised?"

"Why should I be surprised? This is the day you said you'd be back."

"But we— Oh, never mind."

Pat and I had one day to settle into the house and, by the time I was back in my office, it all felt like a dream.

"Welcome home," my boss said. "How was the trip?"

"Incredible. We made an emergency landing in Panama—" I said.

"Hey, that's great. I want to hear all about it. By the way, Dave called and he wants to talk to you as soon as you get settled—"

"We made an emergency landing in Panama," I tried again over coffee with a colleague.

"Really?" he said. "That's interesting. We had a system crash Christmas Day, and I was in here until midnight."

"Don't you see?" I wanted to scream. "You're missing the risks, the dreams— I learned how to live— Don't you understand?"

Of course he didn't. The adventure was over. We were home. Life would flatten into normality.

I was wrong about that, too. Our brush with death over Panama had whetted my appetite for adventure. Recapturing the immediacy of that experience became a life goal. I have yet to succeed, but there has been great joy in the quest.

A distant shot shows the Cherokee doubly dwarfed by two 747's at Panama International.

Joe in the pilot's seat and David navigating from under my yellow towel.

The Cherokee and a DC-3 at the Buenaventura, Colombia airport.